WALKING ROUND WALES

The Giraldus Journey

Also by Shirley Toulson

The Drovers' Roads of Wales
Derbyshire: Exploring the Ancient Tracks
East Anglia: Walking the Ley Lines and Ancient Tracks

SHIRLEY TOULSON

WALKING ROUND WALES

The Giraldus Journey

MICHAEL JOSEPH
London

MICHAEL JOSEPH LTD

Published by the Penguin Group
27 Wrights Lane, London W8 5TZ, England
Viking Penguin Inc., 40 West 23rd Street, New York, New York 10010, USA
Penguin Books Australia Ltd, Ringwood, Victoria, Australia
Penguin Books Canada Ltd, 2801 John Street, Markham, Ontario, Canada L3R 1B4
Penguin Books (NZ) Ltd, 182–190 Wairau Road, Auckland 10, New Zealand

Penguin Books Ltd, Registered Offices: Harmondsworth, Middlesex, England

First published 1988

Typeset in 11/13pt Novarese by Wilmaset, Birkenhead
Printed and bound in Great Britain by
Butler and Tanner, Frome

A CIP catalogue record for this book is available from the British Library
ISBN 0–7181–2885–0

Contents

Acknowledgements

The inset quotations from Gerald's writings are taken from the texts of his *Itinerarium Kambriae* and the *Description Kambriae* edited by Camden and Wharton in the seventeenth century and translated by Sir Richard Colt Hoare in 1806. I have drawn from the 1908 Everyman edition of his work, edited by W. Llewelyn Williams.

The quotations on pages 3 and 6 of chapter one are taken from H. E. Butler's translation of Gerald's *De Rebus a Se Gestis* (Jonathan Cape, 1937). I have naturally consulted that work as well as Henry Owen's *Gerald the Welshman* (Whiting & Co. 1889) and Lewis Thorpe's translation of Gerald's books on Wales, published as a Penguin Classic in 1978.

On a more personal level, I should like to express my appreciation of the help given me both by CADW (Welsh Historic Monuments) and the custodian of Manorbier. I am grateful for the generosity of Tony Carr of Lugwardine, who gave me the run of his library and the benefit of his extensive knowledge of the area around Radnor; and for the time which Father Seamus Cunnan of Cardigan and Father Charles Lloyd of Tywyn gave to my questions about Baldwin's journey through their parishes.

My thanks are also due to Rosemary Antwis of St Dogmaels and to Thomas Rogers of Llangwm for the help which they gave me in Pembrokeshire, and to Mervyn and Margaret Jones who so kindly lent me their cottage at St David's. Many friends walked with me in the course of my *Giraldus Journey*. I should especially mention Roy Lewis who kindly read through the typescript, but they all know how delighted I was to have their company.

Note for Walkers

The outline maps to the walks in this book provide a general guide to the routes, but it would be unwise to embark on any long-distance walk in Wales and the borders without the relevant sheets of the Ordnance Survey maps. For this reason grid references are given to many of the important places mentioned in the text, and in order to avoid confusion the spelling of Welsh place names adopted by the Ordnance Survey has been adhered to throughout.

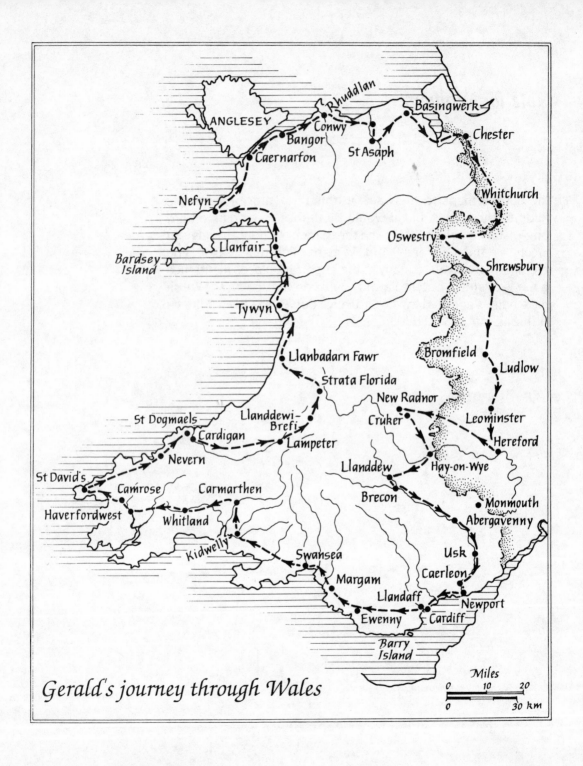

ANGLESEY

Rhuddlan
Basingwerk
Conwy
Bangor
Chester
Caernarfon
St Asaph
Whitchurch
Nefyn
Oswestry
Llanfair
Shrewsbury
Bardsey
Island
Tywyn
Bromfield
Ludlow
Llanbadarn Fawr
Strata Florida
New Radnor
Leominster
St Dogmaels
Cruker
Hereford
Cardigan
Llanddewi-
Brefi
Lampeter
Nevern
Llanddew
Hay-on-Wye
St David's
Camrose
Carmarthen
Brecon
Monmouth
Haverfordwest
Whitland
Abergavenny
Kidwelly
Usk
Swansea
Caerleon
Margam
Llandaff
Newport
Ewenny
Cardiff
Barry
Island

Gerald's journey through Wales

Miles
0   10   20
0   30 km

CHAPTER ONE

Introducing Gerald

Gerald de Barri was in his early forties when, by appointment of Henry II, he set out with Baldwin, Archbishop of Canterbury, on the tour of Wales which took place in 1188. He was a tall, handsome man, whose penetrating, ever-inquiring eyes looked critically at the world from beneath shaggy eyebrows of which their owner was inordinately proud. He was in every way delighted with himself and unflaggingly curious about everything that came his way. His own physical appearance gave him particular satisfaction, and he recalled, with a tinge of sadness for the ravages of time, that when he visited Baldwin at Worcester, long before the latter's elevation to Canterbury, he had been 'a young man and remarkable for beauty of face and form, a boon of nature that endures but for a moment and is gone'.

He never doubted that all the world would be as fascinated by his experiences and opinions in his maturity as it had been charmed by his beauty in youth. His attitude imparts a naive but often endearing arrogance to his writings, but it may well have made him a difficult companion. Likeable or not however, his vitality resonates down the centuries and modern readers of his travel books on Ireland and Wales will find themselves soon agreeing with Professor H. E. Butler (who, in 1937, translated and edited Gerald's autobiography) that the writing is imbued with Gerald's lively personality.

He was born sometime between 1145 and 1147 at Manorbier, to the south of Pembroke, in the castle built by his father, William de Barri. His mother was Angharad, daughter of the Welsh princess, Nest, who was so exceptionally lovely and such a breaker of hearts that she was to become known as the Helen of

Wales. Nest's father was Rhys ap Tewdr, Prince of South Wales, who died in 1093. By that connection, Gerald was related to many of the Welsh princes, his great-grandfather being grandfather to Lord Rhys ap Gruffydd, who was to accompany Baldwin's cavalcade on much of the journey.

Nest bore children to at least two of her lovers, but she married the Norman, Gerald de Windsor, and Angharad was their daughter. Although Gerald had only a quarter of Welsh blood in his veins, his sympathies lay with his grandmother's people, and he was always to be known as Gerald the Welshman. As he served a Norman king, and had many other Norman relations who held land in Wales, he must often have found himself torn by divided loyalties, and this is manifested by some confusion in his writing. He was, however, quite single-minded and clear about his dedication to the church.

He was the youngest of four children, and his older brothers were designed from childhood for the knightly pursuit of establishing and maintaining Norman dominance in Wales and extending it to Ireland. Gerald's path lay in a different direction. From an early age, he was drawn to the church, as he tells the readers of his autobiographical *De Rebus a se Gestis*, in which, as in all his writings, he refers to himself assiduously in the third person:

> When the other three, preluding the pursuits of manhood in their childish play, were tracing or building, in sand or dust, now towns, now palaces, he himself, in like prophetic play, was ever busy with all his might in designing churches or building monasteries. And his father, who often saw him thus engaged, after much pondering, not unmixed with wonder, being moved by this omen, resolved with wise forethought to set him to study letters and the liberal arts, and would oft in approving jest call him 'his bishop'.

The seed was sown. It was wise of William de Barri to dedicate his youngest son to letters, for Gerald was to become one of the most scholarly men of his generation widely read in both Latin and Greek, and quick to quote from the classical authors in order to confirm an argument. His formal schooling started when, as a young boy, he was sent away from the sands of Manorbier to the Benedictine Abbey of St Peter's in Gloucester. Under the instruction of the learned Master Hamo, he grew into so brilliant a pupil, that he was sent on to continue his studies at the University of Paris, hub of western civilization. In all he spent twelve years there. For the first nine, he studied grammar, logic and rhetoric, the three subjects essential for a medieval man of letters. Then after a stormy interval back in Britain, he returned to France to read canon law and theology and to lecture in those subjects for a further three years.

The interval in his studies did not last long, but in that time he came close to achieving the primary ambition of his life, which was to be appointed to the Bishopric of St David's and from that position to free the church in Wales from the authority of Canterbury. When that hope was snatched away from him, he returned to France. However, that was all in the unknown future, when he returned to be ordained and to take up the appointments provided for him by his maternal uncle, the reigning bishop, the very man whom he expected to succeed.

Although he was still under thirty, he had no intention of spending any time as an obscure parish priest. At the very outset he was determined to play a leading part in national church affairs. As a first move, he went to Canterbury in order to draw attention to himself, and while he was there he complained to Richard, the Archbishop, that the Flemish settlers in Pembrokeshire refused to pay the tithes of wool and cheese to the diocese of St David's. Richard's response was to send Gerald back to Wales as his personal representative, with the authority to put things right as best he saw fit, and to instigate reforms which would make for greater discipline within the church as a whole.

Gerald certainly did not stop at the non-payment of tithes. His ideas of reform went into much wider channels. He was always to be a stern advocate of clerical celibacy, and he constantly attacked the tradition, retained by the Welsh church from its earliest days, that married priests were acceptable. One of his first public moves was to make a public example of the wretched Jordan, the elderly, long-married Archdeacon of Brecon, who refused to put his wife aside. As a result of the fuss that was stirred up, Jordan was removed from office, and Gerald became Brecon's archdeacon in his place. He still held that position fourteen years later when he accompanied Baldwin round Wales.

In 1176, Gerald's uncle, Bishop David, died, and the way now seemed clear for his nephew's ambition to be realised. Pre-empting the usual formalities, the chapter promptly nominated Gerald to the See. However the final endorsement was in the hands of the king; and Henry II had every good reason to withhold his consent. He believed that his position in Wales would be seriously threatened if anyone as politically ambitious and as well-connected as Gerald were to become Bishop of St David's. So the king summoned the whole chapter to Westminster, and compelled it, in his presence, to elect Peter de Leia, prior of the Cluniac Abbey of Wenlock. Disgruntled, Gerald returned to Paris where he stayed until 1179, when lack of funds forced him to return home.

Henry's firm intervention in the appointment of the Bishop of St David's was no doubt partly motivated by Gerald's known admiration for the austere and committed life of Thomas à Becket, whose integrity had led to his murder only six years previously. After his exile in France, Becket had lived for a while with the Cistercian monks of Pontigny, and Henry could well have been concerned about Gerald's emphatic advocacy of an order, which unlike that of the Benedictines, warmly welcomed Welshmen into its communities.

Apart from any nationalist feeling, however, Gerald was not entirely without personal prejudice in this matter. At some time he seems to have grown impatient with the Benedictines and Augustinian canons who gave him his early education, for he roundly attacked the foundation at Gloucester when, during the course of his *Itinerary*, he contemplated the history of its mother house at Llanthony. Nor did he have many good words for the Cluniacs, the order to which Peter de Leia, his successful rival for the See of St David's, belonged. He even went so far as to complain that the order was not beyond misappropriating funds, diverting 'to improper uses the largesses which have been collected by divine assistance, and by the bounties of the faithful'. Furthermore the Cluniacs were greedy, and 'sooner than lessen the number of the thirteen or fourteen dishes which they claim by right of custom, or even in a time of scarcity or famine recede in the smallest degree from their accustomed good fare, they would suffer the richest lands and the best buildings of the monastery to become a prey to usury, and the numerous poor to perish before their gates'.

How unlike the Cistercians, who

> *at a time when there was a deficiency in grain, with a laudable charity, not only gave away their flocks and herds, but resigned to the poor one of the two dishes with which they were always contented. . . . This Order, therefore, being satisfied more than any other with humble mediocrity, and if not wholly, yet in a great degree checking their ambition; and though placed in a worldly situation, yet avoiding, as much as possible, its contagion; neither notorious for gluttony or drunkeness, for luxury or lust; is fearful and ashamed of incurring public scandal, as will be more fully explained in the book we mean (by the grace of God) to write concerning the ecclesiastical Orders.*

That book, along with several other projects that Gerald had in mind, was never written, but the number of books that he actually did produce was prodigious. Even in the middle years of his life, while he was absorbed in affairs of state occasioned by his appointment in 1183 as court chaplain to Henry II, his thoughts ran to literature. When Henry commanded him to accompany his son, the eighteen-year-old Prince John on a campaign into Ireland, Gerald made use of the expedition to collect material for his first two books: *Topography of Ireland* and *Conquest of Ireland*. He drew freely on some of the observations on natural history that he made then when he came to write his *Itinerary of Wales* and his *Description of Wales*.

Gerald owed his position at court partly as a reward for the negotiations that he had undertaken on the king's behalf with his cousin Lord Rhys, and partly as a way of keeping him occupied outside Wales. So it is no wonder that he did not hold himself bound by any personal loyalty to Henry II, although he might have felt some restraint had he actually published his Welsh books during the king's lifetime. However Henry died in 1189, at which time Gerald's work was still in note form. He is thought to have completed his first finished version of the *Itinerary* in 1191. By that time he obviously felt free to make it clear to his readers that although his sympathies did not lie wholly with the Welsh, they were certainly not with the English or their king. He took an almost vicious delight in recounting how Henry's sons rebelled against him, and he lost no opportunity to quote prophecies and portents foreshadowing that royal disaster.

His dealings with the Angevin king provided him with material for another book, *De Principis*, an early forerunner of Machiavelli's *Prince*. Indeed he never had any hesitation about using the experiences of his life as material for his books, none of which might ever have been written had he achieved his ambition to become Bishop of St David's. That is not to suggest that he considered authorship a second-best alternative. He never had any qualms about publicising his own work, and when he dedicated a version of his *Description of Wales* to Stephen Langton (Archbishop of Canterbury from 1207), he complained that 'the respect paid to literature vanished with literary princes'. So with royal patronage denied him, it was up to the author himself to make sure that his words were heard, for 'in these degenerate days' nobody was going to seek him out for honour, fame and riches. With that in mind, he arranged a reading of his Irish books

before a great audience at Oxford, where of all places in England the clergy were most strong and pre-eminent in learning. And since his book was divided into three parts, he gave three consecutive days to the reading, a

part being read each day. On the first day he hospitably
entertained the poor of the whole town whom he gathered
together for the purpose; on the morrow he entertained
all the doctors of the diverse faculties and those of the
scholars who were best known and best spoken of; and
on the third day he entertained the remainder of the
scholars together with the knights of the town and a
number of the citizens. It was a magnificent and costly
achievement.

It would be good to know how that venture was greeted by
Gerald's friend, Walter Map of Oxford, another literary archdeacon and also born of a Norman father and a Welsh mother.
Map, who is best known for his satirical writings, was the author
of a cynical work on matrimony, which Chaucer listed as being
among the books consulted by the wife of Bath's fifth husband.
That treatise has been lost to us together with Map's prose
romance of the tale of Sir Launcelot but those writings were
surely known to Gerald, who had his own strong views about the
married state, and who was by no means indifferent to the
fascination of the Arthurian romances, although his main interest was in the character of Merlin, who in one guise or other
makes brief, but frequent appearances in the Welsh *Itinerary*.

Some of the Arthurian references in Gerald's work are drawn
from the work of a slightly earlier author, Geoffrey of Monmouth,
Bishop of St Asaph, who died in 1154 when Gerald was barely
ten. It could have been that Monmouth's *Historia Regum Brittan-
niae* was part of his required reading when he studied as a lad
under Master Hamo of Gloucester. Perhaps it was a dislike of a
school book that caused Gerald to attack that work so viciously in
his own writings, despite the fact that he never hesitated to
quote from it when it suited his purpose.

In doing so, he was not being entirely two-faced, for it was part
of his character to hold strong contradictory opinions about the
same person. In one chapter of the *Itinerary*, he condemns Lord
Rhys for an act 'of the most consummate baseness' in one
paragraph, and in another gives him fulsome praise for his

hospitality to Baldwin. And no sooner has he recounted his own part in the excommunication of Owain Cyfelliog, prince of Powys, at Shrewsbury, than he goes on to praise that man for his 'good management of his territory' and above all for his 'fluent speech'.

He was naturally sympathetic to anybody who could handle language with elegance, for as he confessed in that dedication to Stephen Langton 'the love of letters and the study of eloquence have from my infancy had for me peculiar charms of attraction'. He also had a high regard for precision and accuracy in writing although he confessed that he found 'an accurate investigation of every particular is attended with much difficulty'. Indeed it is hard to believe that he spent much time in attempting to verify the truth of some of the more far-fetched tales that he has to tell, but there is no doubt that a lot of geographical and historical research went into the compilation of both the *Itinerary* and the *Description*.

In an age in which maps were both primitive and cryptic, his topographical descriptions, which list the courses and sources of the major rivers, are outstanding in the clarity of their detail. In his own catalogue of his works, he actually lists a map of Wales which he had drawn to illustrate the *Description*, and he described it in a letter to the chapter of Hereford. As well as rivers and mountains, this map showed castles, cathedrals and monasteries. Sadly it no longer exists, although J. C. Davies, writing in the *Journal of the Historical Society of the Church in Wales* for 1952, notes that it was referred to in 1691 by Henry Wharton in his *Anglia Sacra*. Wharton described a map of Wales, which appeared as the frontispiece to the Westminster Abbey manuscript of Gerald's *Description of Wales*, dedicated not to Stephen Langton but to Gerald's friend and mentor, St Hugh of Lincoln. This work appears in the 1672 catalogue of the Abbey's library, but it seems to have been burnt in the fire that destroyed so many of the books in that building two years later.

It is a sad loss, and one that anybody who tries to sort out some of the discrepancies and difficulties in Gerald's account of his journey is bound to bemoan. At least there is his *Description* to help the traveller in space and time understand the customs and characters of the Welsh as Gerald observed those people; and the *Itinerary* itself is full of glimpses into the lives of ordinary people, as well as the nobles and churchmen whom Gerald travelled with. He was extremely fond of his home at Llanddew in his archdeaconry of Brecon, and he made sure that Baldwin should visit it during the course of his tour.

When he came to write his book, he devoted a whole chapter to the Brecon district. This includes an account of a traditional festival, held in early August at the church of St Almeda, now sadly vanished. Almeda was one of the twenty-four saintly daughters of King Brychan, the legendary figure from whom Brecon gets its name. Each Lammas (August 1st) sick people came to her shrine for healing. At the same time a remarkable, penitential mime and dance took place, when

> you may see men or girls, now in the church, now in the churchyard, now in the dance which is led round the churchyard with a song, on a sudden falling on the ground as in a trance, then jumping up as in a frenzy, and representing with their hands and feet, before the people, whatever work they have unlawfully done on feast days; you may see one man put his hand to the plough, and another, as it were, goad on the oxen, mitigating their sense of labour, by the usual rude song: one man imitating the profession of a shoemaker; another that of a tanner. Now you may see a girl with a distaff, drawing out the thread and winding it again on the spindle; another walking, and arranging the threads for the web; another, as it were, throwing the shuttle and seeming to weave.

The *Description of Wales* tells us how these people lived, what they ate, and even how they cared for their teeth:

> Both sexes exceed any other nation in attention to their teeth, which they render like ivory, by constantly rubbing them with green hazel and wiping with a

> *woollen cloth. For their better preservation, they abstain*
> *from hot meats, and eat only such as are cold, warm or*
> *temperate.*

Gerald must often have experienced Welsh hospitality, and he wrote warmly about the way that guests were entertained, although

> *the kitchen does not supply many dishes, nor highly*
> *seasoned incitements to eating. The house is not*
> *furnished with tables, cloths, or napkins. They study*
> *nature more than splendour, for which reason, the*
> *guests being seated in threes, instead of couples as*
> *elsewhere, they place the dishes before them all at once*
> *upon rushes and fresh grass, in large platters or*
> *trenchers.*

Naturally he wrote about the making of music, explaining that

> *in their musical concerts they do not sing in unison like*
> *the inhabitants of other countries, but in many different*
> *parts; so that in a company of singers, which one very*
> *frequently meets with in Wales, you will hear as many*
> *different parts and voices as there are performers, who*
> *all at length unite, with organic melody, in one*
> *consonance and the soft sweetness of B flat.*

Although he was not Welsh-speaking, and like Baldwin had to make use of an interpreter when he preached to the people in Latin or Norman-French, he had a great affection for the language and a keen interest in its origin and structure. He frequently interrupted the course of his narrative in order to give his readers a lecture in linguistics, demonstrating the Greek origin of many Welsh words. His feeling for the historical importance of the tongue was so strong that it is not surprising to find that he concluded his *Description of Wales* by quoting the panegyric on the immortality of the language, which his cousin

Lord Rhys is supposed to have delivered after he had been defeated by Henry II at Pencader in 1163.

In his journey round Wales, the English Archbishop could not expect that he would always be greeted with the friendliness, hospitality and helpfulness that today's visitors will encounter. Indeed the hostility was such that he was forced to steer clear of the district of Powys, and to make a wide detour on the last stage of his journey south from Shrewsbury in order to avoid that part of the country; and at one point the canons of St David's tried forcibly to prevent his entry into their diocese. Apart from such organised opposition, there was always the danger of an ambush by nationalist extremists or criminal brigands.

So it was a large and well-organised cavalcade that set out from Hereford at the beginning of Lent in 1188. Apart from the body of mounted men accompanying the Archbishop, there were packhorses carrying personal baggage, which in Gerald's case, at least, included books; and the procession included tumbrils and carts filled with provisions. For although the Archbishop was to be handsomely entertained in castles and monasteries during the course of his journey, in many places his men would not be provided for. Most important of all, bales of white cloth had to be taken along. For the whole purpose of the venture was to recruit soldiers for the Third Crusade, and each volunteer had to be given a white cross to sew on his cloak. Gerald made sure that he was the first man on Welsh soil to be so adorned.

CHAPTER TWO

The Journey Starts

The red sandstone of Hereford Cathedral rises out of an island of grass, distancing it from the encroaching and increasingly busy city. It seems a place of timeless peace, yet it grew out of a troubled history. The original stone building was planned by the Saxon Bishop Athelstan to stand on the site of the seventh-century church that housed the healing relics of the saintly Ethelbert, King of East Anglia who had been treacherously murdered by Offa, the pagan ruler of Mercia. From the eleventh century when marauding forces, made up of Danes in unlikely alliance with the Welsh and Irish, destroyed the great stone building, to the shattering collapse of the west tower on Easter Monday, 1786, Hereford Cathedral was in a constant state of alteration and repair.

Hereford and the Marches

Gerald, who was a prebend here before he was thirty, knew the massive Norman pillars, which still support the nave; and as an old man he may have been concerned with the delicate structure of the Lady Chapel, which was completed in 1220. Early in the March of 1188, he was probably more aware of the Bishop's Palace. It stands by the river to the south of the cathedral, and it was there that he and Baldwin spent the night before setting out on their Lenten journey through Wales. It had been newly built, and although that building has now been entirely replaced, the remains of the massive timber arches which supported it are preserved in the porch of the present palace.

Like so many of the places that Gerald and Baldwin were to visit on their travels, Hereford's church history was closely linked to the fortunes of the Norman military defence. When the first cathedral was destroyed in the eleventh century, the Welsh saw to it that the Saxon castle was also obliterated. That was rebuilt by Harold Godwinson in 1063 (some twenty years before the cathedral was restored) and the motte that he raised is now part of the city's public park.

In the next century, when Henry II, with his fellow Christian monarchs, planned the massive war in the Holy Land, the people at home were still in a constant state of rebellion against the Norman overlords. Part of the purpose of Baldwin's tour was to impress the Welsh with the king's authority, and by preaching in the four cathedrals of Llandaff, St David's, Bangor and St Asaph to make it clear that Canterbury was the supreme head of the church in Britain.

That was, as it were, the sub-plot to Baldwin's journey, whose main purpose was to gather recruits for the Third Crusade. The Welsh were renowned fighters. The men of the south, and particularly those of Gwent, were, Gerald contended, especially proficient with the bow and arrow. He gives several examples from the siege of Abergavenny Castle, held by the Norman, William de Braose, to prove his point. Among them was the testimony of de Braose himself, who averred 'that one of his soldiers, in a conflict with the Welsh, was wounded by an arrow, which passed through his thigh and the armour with which it was cased on both sides and, through that part of the saddle which is called the "alva", mortally wounded the horse'.

The northern Welsh, on the other hand, were spearmen, and used their weapons to such effect, Gerald wrote, 'that an iron coat of mail will not resist the stroke of a lance thrown at a small distance'. Henry II looked forward to enjoying a personal triumph when he led such soldiers to the Crusade. Indeed in a letter to Manuel Conmenus, Emperor of Constantinople from 1143 to 1180, whose text Gerald quotes, Henry described the Welsh as being 'so bold and ferocious, that, when unarmed, they did not fear to encounter an armed force; being ready to shed their blood in defence of their country, and to sacrifice their lives for renown'.

By 1188, the contribution of the Welsh to the Holy Wars was urgently needed. In May 1187, Saladin had defeated the Knights Templars and the Hospitallers of St John at Tiberias. Two months later he overwhelmed the united Christian army. On October 2nd, Jerusalem fell to the Saracens. In that same month Pope Urban III died, to be succeeded by Gregory VIII, who only lived until December. Early in 1188, Clement III was elected pontiff and, with his blessing, Henry II with the other ruling heads of Europe rallied their forces to the cause of retrieving the Holy City for Christ. They did so with the same passionate intensity of religious fervour that inspires the fighting Moslems of the twentieth century.

The saintly Cistercian, Bernard of Clairvaux, who died in 1153, best known for his treatise on the love of God, had found nothing strange or contradictory in being equally fervent in preaching the disastrous cause of the Second Crusade. The gentle Baldwin was able to countenance the same discrepancy between encouraging violent military encounters and spreading the peaceable teachings of Christ. We know Baldwin the man through Gerald's description:

> *He was a man of a dark complexion, of an open and venerable countenance, of a moderate stature, a good person, and rather inclined to be thin than corpulent. He was a modest and grave man, of so great abstinence, and continence, that ill report scarcely ever presumed to say anything against him; a man of few words; slow to anger, temperate and moderate in all his passions and affections; swift to hear, slow to speak; he was from an early age well instructed in literature, and bearing the yoke of the Lord from his youth, by the purity of his morals became a distinguished luminary to the people.*

He was clearly a total contrast to the third man who rode out from Hereford on that February day. Rannulf de Glanville, Justicar of England and personal representative of Henry II, was an East Anglian baron, whose fame rests on his treatise concerning the law and practice of the king's court of justice. In his own affairs he was a harsh, and frequently unscrupulous man, who could not tolerate his plans being thwarted. Yet the outwardly gentle and compliant Baldwin was a match for him. Four years previously, when he was still Bishop of Worcester, he had intervened to save the life of a young man whom de Glanville had condemned to death for having the effrontery to marry an heiress, whose wealth had been earmarked for the Justicar's steward.

Gerald has nothing to say about the feelings between himself and his two ill-sorted travelling companions as they set out to ride north-west to New Radnor. Nor does he ever write a word about the state of the weather, declaring it to be unmanly to take note of the elements unless a sea journey is in prospect. He does not even give his readers any descriptions of the places they rode through or mention any distant views. We can only conjecture what he saw, for, in Wales of all places, the views expand and contract with the weather.

New Radnor (OS sheet 148)

We know however that they spent their first night at New Radnor. On a clear day the Welsh hills beckon the traveller journeying from Hereford to the west; and at New Radnor anyone who scrambles up the grassy earthworks that mark the castle where the Archbishop's entourage spent the night can look north and west across the ancient, almost treeless, hunting preserve of Radnor Forest. In New Radnor, the A 44 takes a sharp right-angled bend at the top of the main street to turn into the original village high street. At that bend it forms a junction with the B 4372 from Knighton, and above it the green mound of the castle rises beside the church.

There is no trace now of any stone from that castle. Indeed the main fortifications were probably timber-made, for Radnorshire rock splits easily and is very difficult to handle. The public footpath from the road junction leads to a little-used gate into the churchyard. From there it is possible to climb straight up to the inner of the two castle defences and so on to the grass banks of the 'walls', where the blue and yellow flowers of spring carpet the grass. Here the scents of thyme, bedstraw and meadowsweet fill the air, and peacock butterflies hover about the entrance through which Baldwin, Gerald and Rannulf came into the castle. The only natural delight that is missing here is bird-song. A visitor from across the border might be forgiven for wondering if New Radnor has the same property as Llangorse Lake, of which Gerald had a strange observation to make. He said that the birds around its shores would only sing when a Welshman rode by.

If New Radnor castle shared that property, then the birds would certainly have been in full throat on the Ash Wednesday of 1188. They would not have sung in greeting to Baldwin and Rannulf, and only half-heartedly for Gerald. Their enthusiasm would have been reserved for Rhys ap Gruffydd, prince of South Wales and a cousin of Gerald's through his maternal grand-mother. By a careful manipulation of strategic marriages, com-bined with an uninhibited use of force, Lord Rhys was then in control of all the land from the Tywi to the Dovey. He was to accompany Baldwin through most of that territory and, as one of the most powerful of the Welsh princes, he wanted to make his presence felt at the Archbishop's first night on Welsh soil. It was an important matter, for Baldwin's visit was not entirely welcome, and the canons of St David's even went so far as to try to prevent the Englishman from entering their domain.

To counteract that, Lord Rhys made sure of attending Mass at New Radnor church, when Baldwin made his first recruiting sermon there. With him was Peter de Leia, who had been Gerald's successful rival for the bishopric of St David's two years earlier. It was Gerald, however, who stole the limelight at New Radnor, when with an instinct for the telling dramatic gesture, he made certain that he would be the first man in Wales to volunteer to ride out to the crusade. He ensured that everyone would take note of his gesture by flinging himself prostrate at Archbishop Baldwin's feet. For the rest of the journey round Wales, he wore a white cross sewn to the shoulder of his cloak, a sign that he was bound for the Holy Land. His fellow volunteers were Peter de Leia and Lord Rhys's son-in-law, Einion, prince of Elfael, whose territory ran southwards to the Wye. Lord Rhys declared that he would wait until the Archbishop reached his lands of Deheubarth before he took the cross, but in the event he never did so. His wife,

Gwenllian, who feared the chaos that would ensue at home if her husband were abroad, persuaded him against it.

Immediately after the Mass at New Radnor, Rannulf, no doubt to everyone's relief, returned to England. Baldwin and Gerald continued their journey by travelling the few miles to what Gerald refers to as Cruker Castle. There is some difference of opinion as to which castle Gerald was writing about. Colt Hoare took it to be the castle of Old Radnor, but if he was right it would mean that the Archbishop retraced his steps to the south-east. Although this seems to be unlikely, Old Radnor is worth making a detour for, on its own account, as well as for the remote possibility that one of the two castles in the village was Gerald's Cruker.

Old Radnor

An arc of the bank and moat that served the castle which Colt Hoare probably had in mind, are clearly visible in the field next to the old school building, which is now a private house. It stands opposite the rocky mound on which a church has stood for many centuries. The castle is said to have been built by Harold Godwinson, who used it as a base from which to dominate Mid Wales. However, it has also been claimed that there never was a castle here, and that the earthworks are the remains of a fortified manor house. Those who take that view suggest that the pre-Norman defence of Old Radnor lay in the valley to the north of the village. There, between a stream and a new forestry plantation, are the remains of the oddly-named Castle Nimble. Its low-lying situation makes nonsense of the claim put forward by Colt Hoare that Cruker is a corruption of Crûg-caeran, the mount of the fortifications.

The church, which Baldwin would certainly have visited if he did indeed spend two nights at Old Radnor, was completely replaced in the fifteenth century by the present building, which, however, still contains a seventh-century font, shaped out of a solid piece of igneous rock, left by glacial action in the valley at the end of the last ice-age.

It seems improbable that Baldwin saw it, for there is another derivation for Cruker. The name could come from Crugerydd (the

Castell Crugerydd

mount of the eagles), which is the name of the castle, whose grassy, treeless mound stands a few miles to the west of New Radnor. That castle is in the territory of Maelienydd, the south-westerly division of the country to the north of the Wye. One good reason for equating it with Gerald's Castle Cruker is that he tells us that Maelgwn ap Cadwallon, Maelienydd's prince, took the cross there, a cause of great distress to his followers.

Their concern at Maelgwn's intended departure for Jerusalem was more political than personal. Some forty-five years before the Archbishop's visit, the land of Maelienydd had fallen into the hands of the Norman Mortimers, and ever since that time there had been ceaseless and bloody territorial disputes between the baronial family and the Welsh princes. In 1179, Maelgwn's father had been murdered by a Mortimer, and although the Norman was banished for that deed, and although his estate was forfeited, the threat of further attacks was not much diminished. Indeed in 1195, the murderer returned to Radnor Forest and took up his vendetta against the sons of Cadwallon.

It was around the castle of Crugerydd that these disputes raged. Latter-day antiquarians have described these earthworks as being the most interesting twelfth-century remains in the kingdom. They form a bare grassy mound now, but a few dead stumps of trees still mark the fact that the motte and the defence ditches were once almost obscured by woodland. This castle is a marvellous defensive position. The whole, wide vale of Builth lies open before it to the south, and anyone approaching from the west has to cross the forbidding spine of the rocks of Llandegley.

From New Radnor, the road to Crugerydd castle follows the valley of the Summergil Brook, and no doubt there was some sort of rough track here for the Archbishop to ride along. To the north of the road are the heights of a treeless medieval hunting preserve, Radnor Forest, in which Gerald had several previous adventures.

Walk A: Radnor Forest (OS sheet 148)

It is a good place to walk across now. A couple of miles out of New Radnor (195594) a rough farm road runs above the rich water-meadows fed by a tributary of the Summergil Brook. Where that stream forks, among the conifers of the Warren Plantation, there is a waterfall, with the delightful name of Water-break-its-neck, justified in wet weather when it falls as a steep torrent. If there is any lack of rainfall, it is speedily reduced to an almost indiscernible trickle.

The path through the woods, which leads up to it, is bordered with white valerian that clings to the rocks beneath the trees. Otherwise, as in so many conifer plantations, the place seems almost devoid of life, inhabited only by pestering midges. Beyond the waterfall, the path emerges into open ground to climb round the slopes of Nyth-grug, and run north-west across the contours of the valley. This path must be closely adhered to as the Ministry of Defence owns the land to the east of it and uses it for military purposes.

Historically, this has always been a troubled area. When Gerald rode past it with Baldwin, he must have recalled that it was among these bare, rounded hills that he had once fallen foul of the constant clashes between the Mortimers and the Welsh princes. At that time, he had set out from his archdeaconry at Brecon in order to make a clerical tour of the regions of Elfael and Maelienydd, only to find that the resident clergy were in a frenzy lest their disputes with the secular overlords should be aggravated by Gerald's well-known reforming zeal. In vain, they begged him to delegate another, more amenable, priest to make the tour in his stead.

Doubtless Baldwin had to listen to the whole story as they jogged along. When Gerald declared that he was determined to come in person, the priests had held up a crucifix in front of him hoping to bar his way to the hills, as they warned him of the bands of bowmen who waited in ambush for him. Their threats only strengthened Gerald's determination, but despite his insistence his retainers were eventually driven back by arrows, and the archdeacon himself was ignominiously forced into taking sanctuary in a church. A disgraceful affair altogether!

We do not know what building it was that gave him protection. Perhaps he retreated to Llanfihangel-Nant-Melan on the road west from New Radnor, where a church still stands in the circular churchyard that indicates the pagan and early Christian origin of this sacred site. Whether it was at that place or not that he was forced to shelter, the memory of the incident caused Gerald to recall a similar incident that happened in these parts during the reign of Henry I, and to insert the following anecdote into his account of the first few miles of the Archbishop's tour. The story concerns the Norman lord of Radnor castle and his adventures in the adjoining territory of Builth, when he

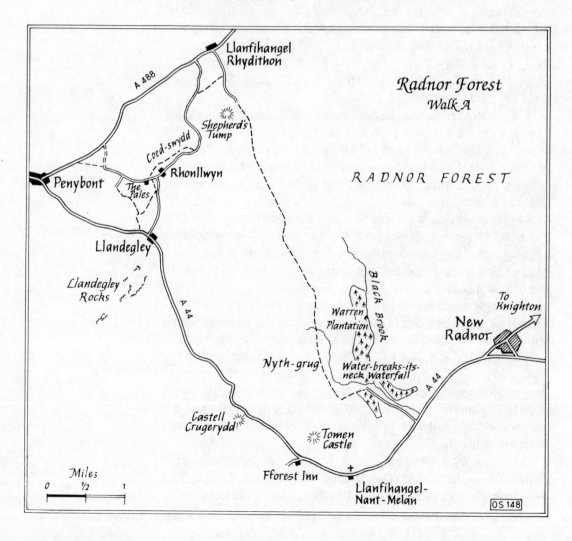

*entered the church of Saint Avan (which is called in the
British language Llann Avan), and, without sufficient
caution or reverence, had passed the night there with his
hounds. Arising early in the morning according to the
custom of hunters, he found his hounds mad, and
himself struck blind. After a long, dark and tedious
existence, he was conveyed to Jerusalem, happily taking
care that his inward sight should not in a similar
manner be extinguished; and there being accoutred,
and led to the field of battle on horseback, he made a
spirited attack upon the enemies of the faith, and, being
mortally wounded, closed his life with honour.*

It is about six miles across the hills to Llanfihangel Rhydithon
which lies on the A 488, the road which runs round the north of
the Forest. The path, across this ocean of empty hills, starts in
the south by following the western contours above the valley,
and then climbs up to higher ground, where it joins a farm track,
through sheep pastures, divided by wire and walls. Just beyond
the barrow of Shepherd's Tump, on the ridge of a small hill a few
yards to the west of the path, the way divides. The wider track
goes steeply downhill to the main road and Llanfihangel
Rhydithon. The 'way less travelled by' turns west to meet the
lane, which twists down towards The Pales, a seventeenth-
century, thatched, Quaker meeting house. There is also a
footpath round the eastern contour of Coed-swydd hill, and that
comes out on to the lane above the farm of Rhonllwyn. Here The
Pales, set on a steep spur of high ground, faces the hills towards
Llandegley.

The south porch of the little building is the entrance to an airy
room, still furnished with the same benches that the Radnorshire
Friends have sat on, in alert silence since 1673. The building
was given to the Society by the farmer at Rhonllwyn, after George
Fox had preached, eloquently and persuasively on Penybont
Common for three hours in 1657.

From The Pales, the track goes west for a couple of miles
across the hill to join the road above Penybont village; and there

are footpaths, from the meeting house, as well as a minor road, running south to Llandegley.

Walk B: By Summergil Brook

The other walk from New Radnor towards Crugerydd castle earthwork follows the Summergil Brook, and goes directly along the higher ground that Baldwin would have ridden over if there had been much flooding on his Lenten journey. Immediately opposite the farm road that goes up to Water-break-its-neck, a sandy track leaves the A 44 main road south to cross the stream, and then climbs steeply uphill across a patch of woodland to meet a well-marked ridgeway. That track goes west to the farm of Foice, and then widens to join the A 481 between Fforest Inn and the desolate, weed-covered swamp of Llynheilyn.

It was in this sinister place that the body of a well-known local character, John Lloyd, the bone-setter, was dumped after he had been attacked and robbed on his return from the Michaelmas Fair at Builth Wells. His corpse was discovered by the daughter of the landlord of Fforest Inn, a circumstance that is still commemorated in the bar there, where a broadsheet spells out the dreadful story.

Walk C: Fforest Inn to Glascwm

Whether it was near here at Crugerydd, or at Old Radnor, to the east, that Baldwin stayed, the next stage of his journey took him south across the River Wye to Gipsy Castle in Hay-on-Wye. Whichever way he went, it was a long day's ride. Gerald gives no indication of the route that was taken, but he does tell two anecdotes about the country they went through. One concerns the church in the village of Glascwm, and the other is about the ominous formation of a new stretch of water, which could well refer to the lake near Painscastle. So it seems reasonable to suppose that wherever the cavalcade set out from, it went south through those places.

Glascwm is certainly on a more direct route from Crugerydd to the south than it is from Old Radnor; from the latter place it would be quite unnecessary to go so far to the west in order to reach Painscastle. From Crugerydd the route is clearer. A walker must start from Fforest Inn, going south over Gwaunceste Hill to

Giants Grave, a tumulus which marks the course of an ancient prehistoric trackway. From there the route descends into Glascwm by a sandy path that reaches the village a little to the east of the church.

An alternative way, is to take the A 481 from Crugerydd to

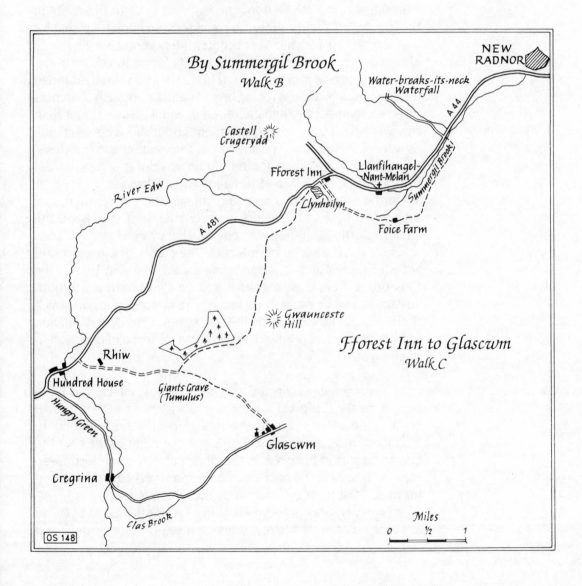

Hundred House and follow the lanes across the open moorland of Hungry Green to cross the Edw at the village of Cregrina. This was the way frequented by the cattle drovers from the seventeenth century. There was a shoeing station in Cregrina, where the animals had iron soles known as 'cues', fitted to protect their cloven hoofs on the long journey to the east.

In the seventeenth century, the last wolf in Wales was shot in these hills. In Gerald's time, the packs were so numerous, that for all his fondness for animal anecdotes, he never mentions a wolf. They were only one of the many hazards facing travellers in the roadless wilderness of Wales, and in these little-visited, rounded hills and marshy valleys roving bandits and an ambush of archers directed against the English prelate posed a greater threat than the wild beasts. Gerald is quite silent about these dangers and, as well as being totally reticent about the weather and the views, he hardly ever mentions the terrain he was riding across, unless the cavalcade actually had to negotiate quicksands.

On the hillside, just above the village of Cregrina, there is a tiny, white-washed thirteenth-century church. It stands on the site of a wattle-built Celtic chapel, which may well have still been in use at the time of Baldwin's tour. The monks of Glascwm said Mass in that church, walking some four miles west beside the Clas Brook, from their monastic cell or 'Clas', from which both stream and village take their name. The remote valley, in which their settlement was established, is surrounded by a confusion of hills, in which it is all too easy to lose all sense of direction in misty weather.

Glascwm

In the nineteenth century, the London post-chaise ran regularly along the turnpike road through Glascwm, and the droves of black cattle were still coming this way in sufficient numbers to warrant a drovers' inn, which supplied overnight grazing for the beasts, to stay in business in the village until the first world war. Now, although many of the old farm tracks have been surfaced for motor traffic, in the main only local people use them.

In February, Glascwm church, which was dedicated to St David at some point in its history, rides on a sea of snowdrops. It is a sight that would make more impression on the nineteenth-century diarist, Francis Kilvert, curate of nearby Clyro, than on Gerald, who had little interest in plants. He was much more concerned about the church's connection with St David, who had been canonised in 1120, and who was firmly established as a symbol of Welsh nationalism. Gerald believed that the church at Glascwm once contained a most holy relic connected with the sixth-century saint. It was no less an object than David's hand-bell, with which he was wont to call the faithful to prayer. Gerald has this story to prove its power:

> At Elevein, in the church of Glascum, is a portable bell, endowed with great virtues, called Bangu, and said to have belonged to Saint David. A certain woman secretly conveyed this bell to her husband, who was confined in the castle of Raidergwy, near Warthrenion, (which Rhys, son of Gruffydd, had lately built) for the purpose of his deliverance. The keepers of the castle not only refused to liberate him for this consideration, but seized and detained the bell; and in the same night, by divine vengeance, the whole town except the wall, on which the bell hung, was consumed by fire.

Raidergwy is Rhayader, a town that marks the northern limit of Radnor Forest, and the area of Warthrenion (together with Maelienydd and Elfael) was bitterly torn by territorial disputes. Elfael, the most southerly of the three districts, lay between Glascwm and the Wye. It was the scene of the next part of the Archbishop's journey.

It was of this area that Gerald tells his tale of the portentous flooding of two hill-top pools:

> It came to pass also in the province of Elevein, which is separated from Hay by the river Wye, in the night in which King Henry I expired, that two pools of no small extent, the one natural, the other artificial, suddenly burst their bounds; the latter, by its precipitate course

*down the declivities, emptied itself; but the former, with
its fish and contents, obtained a permanent situation in
a valley about two miles distant.*

Writing in the sixteenth century, John Leland described 'a llinne in Low Elvel within a mile of Payne's castel by the church called Llanpeder. The llinne is caulid Bougkline, and is of no great quantite, but is plentiful of pike and perche and eles'. That sounds quite like the pool that Gerald had in mind. Llanbedr (Leland's Lanpeder) is, in fact, a good bit more than a mile to the west of Painscastle, and the lake (Llan Bwch-llyn) is a mile further west again. I think however that this is the place, and that the Archbishop's ride south from Glascwm could well have taken him over Rhulen Hill to the rocky, heather-covered shores of the little lake, which Kilvert described as 'lying in its hollow like a silver shield.'

Walk D: Glascwm to Painscastle

Opposite the church in Glascwm, a wide track climbs steeply up to Glascwm Hill, a height of some 1,500 feet. The streams drain east from here, and to that side of the hill there is a blanket of peat in the valley and wide marshy 'mawn' pools. The track continues to the west of Red Hill, and then goes south-west over Rhulen Hill where it turns south to Llanbedr Hill. There is a sharp rocky outcrop beside the track as it goes along that way to a convergence of four paths. After a few yards the one heading to the west divides, the left-hand fork skirts the southern edge of another rocky outcrop, and then runs south towards the lane that goes east to Painscastle past Llewetrog. Llan Bwch-llyn Lake lies in low ground on the other side of that lane.

There is another route to the lane. The path that runs south-east from Llanbedr Hill passes yet another ridge of rock and then enters a steep, green valley. At Pen Cwm, the head of this valley, there is evidence of a long-vanished habitation. Some grassy banks and a few remaining stones outline the small dwelling and garden enclosure, where Kilvert's friend the Reverend Price, the eccentric vicar of Llanbedr, lived alone in squalor among his piles of theological books. There he stayed, suffering a few rare visitors, until he died in 1895 at the age of 85. His grave is still tended in Llanbedr church, three miles away, reached by the farm roads from Penbedw, just below Pen Cwm.

A few yards from Llanbedr church, the lane from Llan Bwch-llyn Lake meets the B 4594 road going into Painscastle. The castle which gives that village its name is marked by an earthwork to the south of the settlement. Here a motte was thrown up by the Norman Payn Fitzjohn in 1130. It was his timbered fortification that Gerald knew, for it was not until the reign of Henry III, that the castle was rebuilt in stone. In that form it has been identified with the Garde Doloureuse of Sir Walter Scott's *The Betrothed*, a novel based on the fearsome battle that took place at Painscastle when Llewellyn the Great was making his bid for Welsh independence. That was by no means the first blood to be spilt there. Long before the stone castle was built, Painscastle was the scene of many fierce fights between the Welsh and the tyrannical Norman, Gerald's contemporary, William de Braose of Abergavenny.

Painscastle

If Baldwin had approached Painscastle from Old Radnor, he would have come to it by the route now covered by the lanes which run through the villages of Bryngwyn and Rhos-goch, and he would still have had steep, wild hills and marshy valleys to negotiate. In March, he might also have been confronted by the sudden sight of the distant, snow-covered sheer escarpment of the north face of the Eppynt range rearing up on the horizon.

Whichever route Baldwin took to Painscastle, the way would have been familiar to Gerald, for de Braose's castle stood in the hills, only four miles north of Llowes, where the archdeacon's spiritual adviser, the holy Wechelau lived as an anchorite. He was a Cistercian monk from the monastery of Abbey Cwmhir to the north, and had been given a dispensation by his order to live a solitary life. Unlike the Reverend Price of Llanbedr, Wechelau was no scholar. It is said that he only learnt to speak Latin, and that in a very rough way without any understanding of the inflexions of the language, after a miraculous intervention occurred as a result of his eating a loaf of bread left on his altar. It

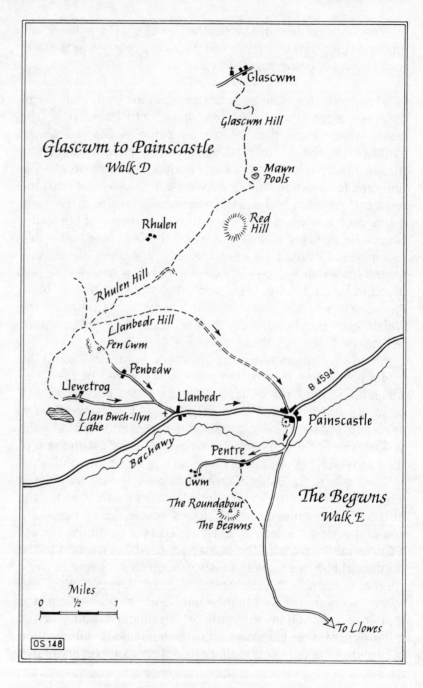

Glascwm

Glascwm Hill

Glascwm to Painscastle
Walk D

Mawn
Pools

Rhulen

Red
Hill

Rhulen Hill

Llanbedr Hill

Pen Cwm

Penbedw

Llewetrog

Llanbedr

B 4594

Llan Bwch-llyn
Lake

Painscastle

Bachawy

Pentre

Cwm

The Roundabout

The Begwns
Walk E

The Begwns

Miles
0   ½   1

OS 148

To Llowes

is a surprisingly pleasing thought that the arrogant Gerald de Barri, one of the finest scholars of his age, should regularly journey across the hills to seek the help and advice of a man who must have seemed to him to be almost illiterate.

The place where Wechelau lived as a solitary recluse, stands at the southern edge of the hills where the water-meadows run down to the Wye. There he dwelt in a small cell attached to the church, beside a tall, double cross dedicated to the Celtic St Meulig. One of the crosses was formed in the seventh century, the other only a hundred years before. For centuries the earlier cross stood on the heights of The Begwns; now the whole pillar has been taken into the church. When Wechelau was here, his Abbey of Cwmhir held a grange close by, and the original monastic archway still stands in a farm wall a little to the north-east of the church.

A lane from Painscastle runs through the rough, bracken-covered heathland that forms the eastern edge of The Begwns. Although this is a fairly small area, it is surprisingly remote. Many of the ways shown as tracks on the Ordnance Survey map have now become maintained roads but it is still quite easy to get lost between them, and bewildered by the interweaving sheep runs, when an apparently green and peaceful paradise suddenly turns into a misty morass. Yet if the weather is clear these hills provide good walking country. After the lane going south from Painscastle crosses the stream of Bachawy, a turn to the right is signposted to Llandewifach church (above Cwm at 146455). That lane goes past the farm of Pentre, where a path starts to climb steeply to the tumulus at the height of The Begwns. There the remains of a wall stand among some freshly planted pines. They mark the building which Kilvert knew as The Roundabout, from which a path runs south-east down the hill to rejoin the lane for Llowes.

Walk E: The Begwns

Somewhere between Llowes and the present village of Clyro, Baldwin and Gerald crossed the Wye and came to Hay. They were not bound for the present hill-top castle in the centre of the

Hay-on-Wye

town, from which, in our own day, Richard Booth plans and rules his kingdom of second-hand and antiquarian books. That castle was initially the work of William de Braose, who built it in 1200. It was to suffer many vicissitudes. In 1231, it was burnt down by Llewellyn, only to be restored by Henry III some two years later. That building was finally destroyed by the Welsh in the fifteenth century. For two hundred years the site appears to have remained derelict, and then a grand mansion was set up in the castle ruins.

Gipsy Castle, the name that is given to the motte, where Baldwin spent the one night that he stayed in Hay, has long been reduced to a simple green mound, rising symmetrically between the much-restored church and the cattle market. There, in the early spring of 1188, in what was then a fairly simple fortification and stockade beside the river, the men who had been persuaded to take the cross sought refuge from their relations who struggled to prevent their action. For despite his long ride across the hills, immediately he came to Hay Baldwin preached to such effect that he drew many volunteers to his cause, even though their desperate friends tore at their garments in a vain attempt to prevent them from going forward. Baldwin's officials had to deal with a host of frantic, half-naked, but determined recruits, thronging the bailey of the castle, before they could go to their own brief rest.

CHAPTER THREE

From the Wye to the Usk

Early next morning, they set out from Hay towards Brecon, where the Archbishop was to preach again. Their way went west along the south bank of the Wye, and then turned south, following the course of the Llynffi to Bronllys, the Court of Rushes. In that place, a castle has stood since the Normans first penetrated the Welsh borders. The original wooden fortification on the motte raised by Bernard de Newmarche was destroyed by fire in 1175; and the round, stone tower which replaced it is all that now remains of the castle that Walter Clifford set here in the mid-thirteenth century. By means of a wooden stairway, it is still possible to enter the first floor of that tower which, like most defensive buildings of its day, had no doors or windows below that level.

Bronllys (OS sheet 161)

At Bronllys, they turned to the west, riding by the waters of the Dulas towards Llanddew, where Gerald had his dwelling as Archdeacon of Brecon. It was a place he loved, saying of it:

Llanddew (OS sheet 160)

> In these temperate regions I have obtained (according to the usual expression) a place of dignity, but no great omen of future pomp or riches; and possessing a small residence near the castle of Brecheinoc, well adapted to literary pursuits, and to the contemplation of eternity. I envy not the riches of Croesus; happy and contented with that mediocrity, which I prize far beyond all the perishable and transitory things of this world.

Llanddew, a growing village a couple of miles to the north-east of Brecon, still retains a vestige of Gerald's dwelling just opposite the church. His 'small residence' was, in fact, a minor castellated palace belonging to the diocese of St David's. All that is left of it now is a few yards of wall and some ruined stones in a tiny garden, which also includes a fourteenth-century archway. By the sixteenth century, as Leland tells us, the palace was already an 'unsemeeli ruin'. Much later the grounds provided space for a vicarage, which has now become a guesthouse, whose lawns spread over the place where Gerald followed his literary pursuits and worked on the notes of his *Itinerary through Wales*.

His church stands on slightly raised ground to the west of his dwelling. For all his love of St David, he was adamant that the name of Llanddew came from 'the Church of God', although the present cruciform building, which Gerald may well have had a hand in designing, is dedicated to the national saint of Wales, and 'Dew' most likely derives from 'Dewi'. In the massive nineteenth-century south porch, there is a small token of the building that Gerald knew when he first took up his residence here in 1175. The lintel above the massive door is inscribed with the rough date 'About 1020 AD'. The piscina in the south transept is another relic of that early church. Everyone stepping through the doorway now is immediately greeted by a newly-designed effigy of Gerald, which dominates the north wall of the nave.

Walk A: Llanddew to Brecon

From the church, the lane going west from the crossroads, which form the centre of Llanddew village, runs beneath the walls that were once a part of Gerald's house. Beyond the walls are the stones surrounding the fourteenth-century wells, which provided both the resident prelate and the villagers with their water supply. Now the lane goes on past farm buildings to run downhill to the Honddu. On the eastern side of the bridge, by which the lane crosses the river, a muddy footpath runs south beside the Honddu as far as the A 4062, whose high banks support colonies of spotted orchis.

Here a footbridge crosses the river, beside a building which stands on the site of the old ironworks' forge. Across the water, the path enters a nature reserve offering a choice of woodland

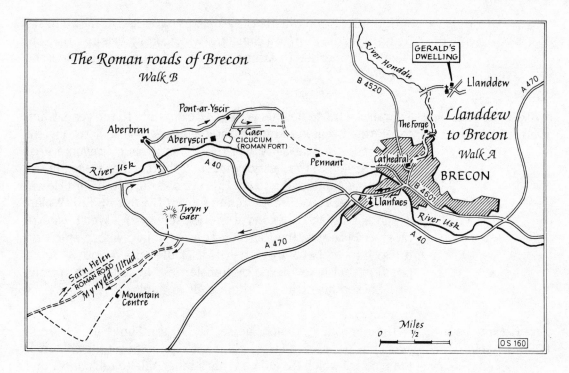

tracks leading to the playing fields in front of the church which became the cathedral of Brecon in 1923.

Brecon Cathedral

This building stands on the site of the church which served the priory founded by Bernard de Neufmarche, a Norman baron who wrenched the land of Brecknock from Bleddyn ap Maenarch some thirty years after the Conquest. In the first decade of the thirteenth century, William de Braose, whose religious fervour existed alongside a brutal insensitivity to the Welsh, planned a great new church above the Honddu. It stood high above the river beside Bernard de Neufmarche's castle, whose ruins now lie in hotel grounds. Below it is Brecon town, and to the south-west, the vast Norman hunting preserve of Fforest Fawr, a wild mountainous region running into the red heights of the Brecon Beacons to the east, which Gerald knew as Cadair Arthur, or

Arthur's Seat, and which he tells us was 'so called from two peaks rising up in the form of a chair, and which, from its lofty situation, is vulgarly ascribed to Arthur, the most distinguished king of the Britons'.

Walk B: The Roman roads of Brecon

To walk on those heights is to go back in time to the years when the Roman legions applied their engineering skill to ancient prehistoric trackways. Two of the Roman roads converge near Trecastle well to the west of Brecon; a third can be traced in the hills to the south of the town. This is a section of the Sarn Helen, part of a network of roads running from North to South Wales, which according to legend were devised by the Welsh wife of Magnus Maximus, the fourth-century Spaniard whose ambition drove him to become emperor of Gaul, Britain and Spain, a position that he achieved by transferring those Roman legions who backed his claim in Britain over to Gaul.

Sarn Helen to Y *Gaer* *(OS sheet* 160)

The only way to reach the section of the Sarn Helen nearest Brecon is to cross the Usk by the A 40 leading past the church of Llanfaes, of which Gerald had this strange tale to tell concerning a boy who tried to take some young pigeons out of their nest in the church eaves. His hand

> *adhered to the stone on which he leaned, through the miraculous vengeance, perhaps, of that saint, in favour of the birds who had taken refuge in his church; and when the boy, attended by his friends and parents, had for three successive days and nights offered up his prayers and supplications before the holy altar of the church, his hand was, on the third day, liberated by the same divine power which had so miraculously fastened it. We saw this same boy at Newbury, in England, now advanced in years, presenting himself before David the Second, bishop of St David's, and certifying to him the truth of this relation, because it had happened in his diocese. The stone is preserved in the church to this day*

among the relics, and the marks of the five fingers
appear impressed on the flint as though it were in wax.

To the west of the church, a lane climbs up to the boggy commonland of Mynydd Illtud, where herds of wild ponies graze the hillocks of rough wet grassland, and splash through marshes white with water crowsfoot. The Sarn Helen runs to the north-west of the Brecon Mountain Centre, and a short stretch of it can be discerned beside a little plantation of pines (966262). This was the road that once ran past the Roman fort of Twyn Y Gaer to the great fort of Cicucium on the opposite bank of the Usk. It is not possible to follow the course of the Sarn Helen for more than a few yards, and Cicucium must be reached now by a twisting network of lanes. A square embankment clearly marks the outline of this massive auxiliary fort, whose stone-faced earthen walls were protected by two fifteen-foot-wide ditches. The massive gateway in each wall can still be traced, although the one to the north is somewhat obscured by the present farm buildings. From the lane leading to that farm, a track goes west into Brecon, entering the outskirts of the town by the side of the old railway cutting. From here a minor road goes to the north side of the town bridge across the Usk.

It was from there that the Archbishop set out on the next stage of his journey to Abergavenny. He had spent two nights at Gerald's dwelling in Llanddew, preaching in the church there and at the priory in Brecon, although there is no mention in Gerald's *Itinerary* of the recruits that came forward as a result of his eloquence in these parts. Perhaps that was because Gerald found it more interesting to record how he supplemented his duties as host by presenting Baldwin with a copy of 'his work on *The Topography of Ireland*, which he graciously received, and either read or heard a part of it read attentively every day during his journey; and on his return to England completed the perusal of it'.

It is easy to imagine the proud author questioning Baldwin on his portion for the day, as the entourage turned east out of

Llanhamlach (OS *sheet* 161)

Brecon, following the course of the Wye to Llanhamlach, of which tiny village Gerald had a tale of animal miscegeny to tell. It was a subject that held an irresistible fascination for him, so he interrupts his account of the journey to let his readers know that when St Illtud, the great sixth-century abbot, sought to live in retreat here from the cares of his south coast monastery and college 'the mare that used to carry his provisions to him was covered by a stag, and produced an animal of wonderful speed, resembling a horse before and a stag behind'.

Just past Llanhamlach, the Archbishop's guides surprisingly led him away from the river, over the hills to Llangorse Lake. It was a roundabout route; perhaps it was taken because the river was in flood, or because of the danger from hostile Welshmen who may have been planning an ambush beyond the pass of Bwlch, for they were travelling through territory which Gerald described as being in a state of constant turbulence, recording that 'the natives of these parts, actuated by continual enmities and implacable hatred, are perpetually engaged in bloody contests'.

Tretower Castle

A clue to both the natural and human dangers that lay in wait for a twelfth-century traveller along the Usk valley can be found in the substantial ruins of the castle of Tretower (184214). Here a round stone tower still stands on the motte raised above marshy ground watered by a tributary of the Usk. The ruined walls of the twelfth-century stone keep replace the earlier timber fortifications set in place by Picard, a follower of Bernard de Neufmarche.

In the early fourteenth century, a residential court house grew up beside the castle walls. It was to be gutted during the uprisings of Owen Glendower. In 1450, it was rebuilt by Roger Vaughan, linked by marriage to Picard's descendants. By the seventeenth century, the substantial manor which he created was inhabited by his direct descendant, Charles Vaughan, uncle of Henry Vaughan, physician and metaphysical poet, whose grave lies beneath a yew tree in the church of Llansantffraed beside the Usk, where his brother once held the living.

That man of letters makes a strange contrast to Gerald. Both men were compulsive writers, both were outstanding scholars in their generation, but the arrogance of the archdeacon contrasts strangely with the modesty of the doctor, whose tomb slab bears the epitaph, which he himself composed. It seeks God's mercy for a 'servus inutile, peccator maxime'.

The young Henry Vaughan went to school at Llangattock, on the south bank of the Usk, across the river from Crickhowell. During Stephen's reign a church was built here on the site where the sixth-century St Cadoc had settled. He was reputed to be the son of one of the many saintly daughters whom hagiographical legend ascribes to King Brychan, from whom Brecon got its name. Much of that building can still be traced in the stones of the present parish church.

Llangattock

To get a clearer view of the whole of the Usk valley, and the choice of routes that confronted Baldwin's guides between Brecon and Abergavenny, it is only necessary to climb past the cave-riddled, limestone cliffs above Llangattock village, and onto the peat blanket that covers the high ground of the Mynydd Llangatwg.

Walk C: The Cliffs of Mynydd Llangatwg

From the church, a lane climbs up to the farm of Pencilau and the land which belongs to the Craig y Cilau nature reserve. A path runs under the cliffs here and across an almost barren scree slope. Beyond the scree are the remains of eighteenth-century quarries which provided the limestone used by the new agricultural improvers. This stone was taken down the hillside in containers geared to a double-incline plane, manipulated by a winch whose circular base is still visible. As the needs of industry superceded those of agriculture, the iron, which also exists in these cliffs, was taken south over the hills to Port Talbot.

From the cairn (205143) on the highest point of Mynydd Llangatwg the subsequent developments of this industry dominate the skyline, and fill the valleys to the south. It all came about as Gerald prophesied it would, when he reflected on the rock of Goldcliff, which stands above the Severn to the east of the Usk estuary. The sight of that prominence led him to quote some untraceable classical author writing on the hidden treasures of nature, an observation with which he was in complete agreement:

> *Nor can I be easily persuaded that nature hath given such splendour to the rocks in vain, and that this flower should be without fruit, if anyone would take the pains to penetrate deeply into the bowels of the earth; if any one, I say, would extract honey from the rock, and oil from the stone. Indeed many riches of nature lie concealed through inattention, which the diligence of posterity will bring to light; for as necessity first taught the ancients to discover the conveniences of life, so industry, and a greater acuteness of intellect, have laid open many things to the moderns.*

Useless, but tempting, to speculate as to how he would feel could he know of the tides of industry that submerged the Welsh valleys, and of the near-unbearable problems that have arisen as that tide receded. More comfortable to turn to the north and return to the twelfth century in order to observe the terrain that Baldwin rode through on his way to Abergavenny. From here the route he discarded through the wide vale of the Usk is clearly seen and beyond it the folds of the Black Mountains, which he chose to cross. In dry weather it is possible to make a circular walk from the viewpoint on Mynydd Llangatwg, crossing the boggy ground and returning to Pencilau along the top of the limestone ridge.

In March the Black Mountains still hold their snowfields, and undoubtedly they would have done so when Baldwin took his Lenten way through their steep valleys. To reach those heights from Brecon he had to go round the shore of Llangorse Lake. Now the lane reaches the southern lakeside, where the dull, nineteenth-century church of Llangasty-Talyllyn marks the place where another early Celtic missionary, St Gastyn, founded his settlement or 'llan'. When he came here, he may well have settled

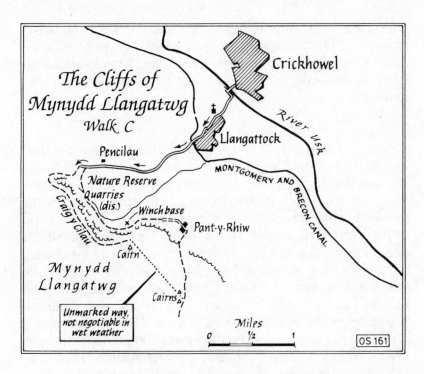

The Cliffs of
Mynydd Llangatwg
Walk C

Crickhowel

Llangattock

River Usk

Pencilau

Nature Reserve
Quarries
(dis.)

Winch base

Pant-y-Rhiw

Craig y Ciliau

MONTGOMERY AND BRECON CANAL

Cairn

Mynydd
Llangatwg

Cairns

Unmarked way,
not negotiable in
wet weather

Miles

0   ½   1

OS 161

by a wild and beautiful stretch of the water, where a family or two still lived on the crannog, or artificial island, at its northern end.

Right through the Middle Ages, when that island settlement had given rise to stories of a submerged city, whose walls and roofs glinted when the sun sent rays slanting through the surface of the water, Llangorse was a particularly rich fishing ground. In Gerald's time it was supplying the country 'with pike, perch, excellent trout, tench and eels'.

Llangorse Lake

Many legends grew up around this lake, including the one re-told by Gerald, that the birds here would only sing when the rightful owner of the land rode by. In addition to that, Llangorse was supposed to be bottomless and to keep its waters unmixed with those of the Lynfi, which flows through it. Gerald wrote that the surface sometimes turned bright green, but since the lake is now a favourite boating and holiday resort, the weed he was no doubt referring to has been kept clear, although banks are still so reedy that the water is well out of sight from the path which goes round the western shore.

Trefeca

From the village of Llangorse to the north of the lake, the road follows the east bank of the Lynfi as it flows towards the Dulas. The way that the Archbishop went passed by the motte, which defended the valley at Trefeca, a village which plunges the modern traveller back into the eighteenth century and the world of the Calvanistic Howell Harris. A life-long Anglican, whose reforming zeal brought him into bitter conflicts with his church, he had much in common with Gerald's austere Catholicism. Like the twelfth-century archdeacon, Harris was a brave man, who even had to suffer physical attacks for his outspoken opinions. The dangers did not deter him, and in 1748 he founded a community at his home and birthplace of Trefeca. There families lived together, pooling their resources and pursuing their individual trades in addition to farming some 800 acres. Harris took a keen and practical interest in the agricultural innovations of his day, and found time from his evangelical activities to take a part in the formation of the Brecknockshire Agricultural Society.

In 1873 a memorial chapel was built to his memory, and now a museum stands beside it displaying aspects from the life of the community, which soon petered out after his death in 1773. However, the college, which he established with the Countess of Huntingdon's aid in the 1760s, still exists as a Christian residential centre.

Talgarth Church

A couple of miles to the north of Trefeca the waters of the Ennig and the Ellyw converge at the pretty little market town of Talgarth. The parish church, in which for all his dissenting ways, Howell Harris was buried, stands on a hill to the east of the town. From here an avenue of ancient yew trees marks the pilgrims' way to the shrine of the little-known St Issui at Patrishow (Patricio) in the southern foothills of the Black Mountains. That route runs through the steep, western valley cut through the hills, which Gerald knew as a 'narrow, woody tract, called the bad pass of Coed Grono'.

He had nothing to say about pilgrims or pilgrimages then, or at any other stage in the course of his writing. Presumably that was because they were as common and as accepted a part of life to him as container lorries and motorways are to us, and so tedious of comment. However, he makes it quite clear that the Archbishop chose to make his way along a route that was both hallowed by holy use and reasonably safe for the traveller on account of the amount of traffic that went along it.

Walk D: Talgarth to Patrishow

From Talgarth church, the pilgrims' way goes north-east through Park Wood to Ffostyll farm, where it joins the lane. From there a path climbs over the heights of Y Dâs and down into the Grwyne Fawr valley. That seems to be the way Baldwin took, but it is not the best route to follow now for it leads straight to the dead waters of a reservoir, from whose dam a road plunges into the extensive depths of the Forestry Commission's Black Mountain Forest, a plantation of dark conifers that has drowned the old Welsh farmsteads as surely as the reservoir has altered the landscape of the valley.

It makes better sense now to go further north-east from Y Dâs and climb over the hill to the head of the valley of Nant Bwch (224345) leading towards Llanthony Priory, a place well-known to Gerald, although there is no proof that Baldwin ever went there. Further to the north-east the path that runs beneath the rocky outcrops on the ridge goes towards Lord Hereford's Knob and the Gospel Pass, which gets its name from the legend that St Peter and St Paul came north across the mountains here on their way to preach to the Welsh at the invitation of the daughter of Caractacus. The story either grew up after Gerald's time, or proved too much for even his easy credulity. He makes no mention of it.

**The monastery of
Father Ignatius**

From the Gospel Pass the road winds down to the banks of the Honddu and the northern end of the Vale of Ewyas at Capel-y-ffin (the chapel at the end of the valley). However a better way to reach that tiny, white-washed church is to take the path to the south-west of the Knob and follow the course of the Nant Bwch down the hillside. Just south of the lane that leads to the road junction and the place where the two streams meet, a rough track climbs up the hillside to a low-lying white building, set up as a 'monastery' in 1869. Its founder was one Joseph Leycester Lyne, a Church of England deacon and maverick of the Oxford Movement, who styled himself 'an Evangelistic Monk of the British Church' and had his followers refer to him as Father Ignatius of Llanthony.

After his death in 1908, his 'monastery' was used intermittently by Roman Catholic monks on retreat from their duties on Caldey Island. In 1924 another Catholic, the artist Eric Gill, stonecarver, calligrapher and type designer, took over the building in order to found a small craft-orientated community where he could settle with his family and friends. During the four years that he lived on this hillside, he attracted many artists to the Black Mountains including the poet and painter David Jones.

A footpath from the monastery gardens goes up the hill beside a small patch of woodland, leading across a marshy piece of ground to the start of a zig-zag climb to the cairn on the ridge between the two valleys. Just past the triangulation point, some two and a half miles to the south along this ridge, another path slants downhill to the road that runs by the ruins of Llanthony Priory.

Llanthony

Gerald made a chapter-long digression from his account of Baldwin's route in order to write of the Vale of Ewyas and to mourn the decline of the monastic ideals which had once prevailed at Llanthony. Possibly his concern about the priory dated from the days of his own schooling at its daughter house which became St Peter's Abbey in Gloucester. As a youth he too may have been sent for a holiday to these hills.

He tells us what the Black Mountain abbey church of St John

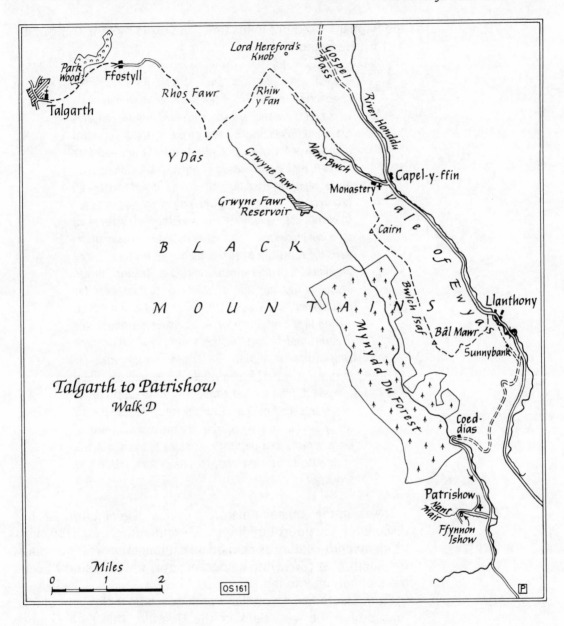

Park Wood

Ffostyll

Talgarth

Lord Hereford's Knob

Gospel Pass

River Honddu

Rhos Fawr

Rhiw y Fan

Y Dâs

Grwyne Fawr

Nant Bwch

Capel-y-ffin

Monastery

Grwyne Fawr Reservoir

Cairn

B L A C K

M O U N T A I N S

Vale of Ewyas

Llanthony

Bwlch Isaf

Mynydd Du Forest

Bâl Mawr

Sunnybank

Talgarth to Patrishow
Walk D

Coed-dias

Patrishow

Nant Mair

Ffynnon Ishow

Miles

0   1   2

OS 161

P

the Baptist looked like in his time, and explains something of its history. He found it:

> *covered with lead, and built of wrought stone; and, considering the nature of the place, not unhandsomely constructed, on the very spot where the humble chapel of David, the Archbishop, had formerly stood decorated only with moss and ivy; a situation truly calculated for religion, and more adapted to canonical discipline, than all the monasteries of the British Isles. It was founded by two hermits, in honour of the retired life, far removed from the bustle of mankind, in a solitary vale watered by the river Hodeni . . . Owing to its mountainous situation, the rains are frequent, the winds boisterous, and the clouds in winter almost continual. The air, though heavy, is healthy; and diseases are so rare, that the brotherhood, when worn out by long toil and affliction during their residence with the daughter, retiring to this asylum, and to their mother's lap, soon regain their long-wished-for health . . . A place truly fitted for contemplation, a happy and delightful spot, fully competent, from its first establishment, to supply all its own wants, had not the extravagence of English luxury the pride of a sumptious table, the increasing growth of intemperance and ingratitude, added to the negligence of its patrons and prelates, reduced it from freedom to servility.*

It was, in the course of history, to suffer degeneration. At the dissolution the priory buildings were sold outright for £160, and its eighteenth-century owner had no compunction about turning the south-west tower into a shooting box, which has now been transformed into an inn.

From Llanthony, a woodland path goes above the lane which runs beside the west bank of the Honddu. This path climbs gradually away from the river as it goes south, until it turns (284243) steeply uphill to Coed-dias, the Wood of Revenge, which gets its name from the revenge that the Welsh took on the Norman baron Richard de Clare, when he came here in over-confident mood in 1135. Gerald tells us what happened, when he fearlessly dismissed his attendants

and proceeded on his journey unarmed; from too great a presumption of security, preceded only by a minstrel and a singer, one accompanying the other on the fiddle. The Welsh awaiting his arrival, with Iorwerth, brother of Morgan of Caerleon, at their head, and others of his family, rushed upon him unawares from the thickets, and killed him and many of his followers.

Just beyond the northern edge of the wood, a bridge crosses the Grwyne Fawr to join the road as it emerges from the Mynydd Du Forest. The pilgrim route to Patrishow now follows the west bank of the river to the point at which a farm track runs towards St Issui's church, and the holy well (Ffynnon Ishow) that springs up in the banks of the woodland stream beneath it.

Hardly anything is known about the saint to whom this enchanting and carefully restored medieval church is dedicated. The story goes that he was a hermit, killed by an ungrateful traveller who had accepted the hospitality of his cell, and that he manifested miraculous healing powers after his death. The first church to stand in this place is said to have been built with the money given for that purpose by a wealthy continental traveller who received a cure for his leprosy after bathing his sores in waters of St Issui's well. The chapel in the west wall of the present church is thought to date from the eleventh century and to be part of that building, which was also the one in which Baldwin celebrated Mass.

St Issui's Church at Patrishow

For although Patrishow's chief glory now is the intricately carved fifteenth-century wooden rood-screen, which was happily preserved from the ravages of Cromwell's men, the main interest for anyone following Gerald's route must be the churchyard cross from which Baldwin is said to have preached the Third Crusade. Unlike the screen, the cross was partly destroyed in obedience to the command of 1547, which forbade the retention of such 'idols'. A more tolerant time has now adorned the remnants of that medieval cross with a crucifix surrounded by the figures of Our Lady flanked by St Issui and the twelfth-century Archbishop.

The Holy Well

It could be, however, that his sermon was not delivered outside the church, for as he rode on his way south he passed St Issui's well. This little spring has long been preserved in a little stone shrine which flows into the Nant Mair, the woodland stream of St Mary. Offerings of wild flowers are still placed in the little niche, where the saint's image once stood. Above the well, on the verge between the road and the stream, a flat unobtrusive piece of rock, inscribed with a Maltese Cross, can be found. Some say that this stone marks the goal of the pilgrims' quest, and that it was here, and not in the churchyard, that Baldwin preached.

Gerald, however, has nothing to say about St Issui's well which is now so delightfully remote or about the journey to Abergavenny. He was anxious to get on with the next part of the story, and to write, as diplomatically as he could, of the atrocities committed by his powerful Norman neighbour, William de Braose, known to folklore as the Ogre of Abergavenny.

It is just possible that Gerald may have deliberately decided that he would not write about Patrishow because the story of Issui's murder was such a close parallel to the outrage against the laws of hospitality which de Braose perpetrated in his castle in Abergavenny in 1175. The story is a reversal of what occurred at Patrishow when a guest slew his host, and of the notorious massacre of Glencoe when the same awful betrayal of trust took place, although it was on the scale of the latter atrocity. At Abergavenny it was the guests who were murdered, in a fearful onslaught taken to avenge the death of William de Braose's uncle, who had been killed by the Welsh led by Seisyll ap Dyfnwal.

On the excuse of working out a peace between the Normans and the Welsh, William invited Seisyll and the other Welsh leaders to a great dinner in his castle. They came in good faith, and as they feasted, unarmed, in the Norman's hall, they were brutally set upon and murdered out of hand. Not content with that carnage, de Braose's retainers ravaged Seisyll's lands, killed his son and imprisoned his wife.

That happened in the same year that Gerald came to Llanddew as archdeacon of Brecon, and it must have caused him immense distress. Yet although he found no problem in attacking married clergy, and what he saw as abuses within the church, he found it almost impossible to rail openly against his neighbour, the powerful Norman overlord. So he argued himself into believing that William 'was not the author of the crime we have preferred passing over in silence, but the executioner, or, rather, not the preventer of its execution, while the murderous bands were fulfilling the orders they had received, de Braose was precipitated into a deep foss, and being taken by the enemy, was drawn forth, and only by a sudden effort of his own troops, and by divine mercy, escaped uninjured'.

In the first version of his *Itinerary*, Gerald did allow himself to be unequivocally censorious of de Braose, but later he toned his comments down, and even added a fulsome recommendation to the Norman baron's sentimental religiosity, and that even after he, as archdeacon, had taken William to task for misappropriating church property. For, he had to say this in his favour, that 'he always placed the name of the Lord before his sentences, saying, "Let this be done in the name of the Lord; let that be done by God's will; if it shall please God, or if God grant leave; it shall be so by the grace of God." '

Naturally, Seisyll's kinsmen were not as tolerant as Gerald. The atrocity at Abergavenny did not stay unavenged. Seven years after the massacre, the sons of the murdered Welsh attacked and occupied the castle in de Braose's absence. For all his apparent refusal to be partisan, Gerald recounted that episode with relish, and expounded on the skill and valour of the Welsh bowmen who had made it possible.

Abergavenny   When Baldwin preached the cross at Abergavenny, having spent the night either in de Braose's reoccupied castle, or as a guest in the Benedictine priory, many of these indomitable archers volunteered to fight in the Holy Land.

The ruined curtain walls of de Braose's castle, and of the later fortification, which Leland was able to describe as a 'fair castle' with 'most goodly towers', are now part of a gentle town park, which accommodates a nineteenth-century building, housing a museum of Victorian bygones, on the site of the Norman motte. There is nothing sinister about this place now. Even on a cold, grey day, the spirit of de Braose does not intrude.

The Priory Church   There is even less left of the priory. Its chapel has now become the parish church of St Mary, whose west front was completely restored in the nineteenth century. Apart from those times when services are being held here, it is only possible to see the medieval interior of this building on a Friday morning when the cleaners are at work. It is worth a visit, if only for the sake of the delightful wooden figure of Jesse supporting the Biblical genealogical tree. Among the many thirteenth-century tombs and effigies here, is that of Eva de Braose, whose husband, William's grandson, was executed in 1229 for taking one of King John's illegitimate daughters as mistress.

The tower of this church, now completely rebuilt, dominates the town as its predecessor did, when Baldwin left Abergavenny by riding south across the Usk. In 1798, Turner painted the Abergavenny bridge of his time, and although the red cattle in that painting would seem strange to twelfth-century eyes, the wild hills were still as empty and forbidding two hundred years ago as they must have seemed on that early Lenten journey.

Baldwin's eyes were set on the way ahead for, as Gerald notes, the Archbishop was anxious to hurry on to Usk. A week had gone by since he had left Hereford, and still he had not preached in any of the four Welsh cathedrals. At Usk, he was to be met by William Saltmarsh, Bishop of Llandaff, who was to accompany him through that diocese, and by Alexander, Archdeacon of

Bangor, who was to interpret his words for the benefit of the Welsh. Indeed, Alexander was to render the same service to Gerald, who spoke only Latin and Norman French despite his royal Welsh blood.

Unless the river is in flood, it is possible to pursue Baldwin's journey from Abergavenny to Usk, by taking the Usk Valley Walk, a series of intermittent footpaths beside the river, which start at the point where the A 4042 crosses it at Great Hardwick, and then follows its westward meanders until it turns south to the charming little market town that bears its name. The Archbishop's entourage may well have entered Usk from the east bank of the river, having taken a route that runs along the contours of the hills above the water-meadows, whereas today's official walkers' way goes by the western bank, reaching the town by the bridge that leads to the castle.

Walk E: Along the Usk Valley (OS sheets 161 and 171)

The ruins of that building stand in private land, but the owners have graciously made it possible for serious visitors, who are prepared to make an appointment by writing to Castle House, to walk round the remains at their leisure. The twelfth-century keep is still standing, a magnificent square tower. It had only been in place for eighteen years when Baldwin stayed here, having been planned and built by Richard Strongbow, a descendant of the de Clare who was murdered in the Black Mountains. His stone fortification replaced a wooden castle that had stood for a hundred years on the long-deserted site of an important Roman base-camp.

Usk Castle (OS sheet 171)

Further additions were to be made to the castle in 1189, when the building began to take on the form that is outlined by today's ruined walls, which are now enhanced by superbly tended gardens, whose ordered delights create a studied informality, accentuated by some magnificent large-scale topiary. The detailed plans of the ruins and the short history of the castle that its owners have kindly prepared for the visitor cannot convey the full charm of the place and the timeless atmosphere, oddly

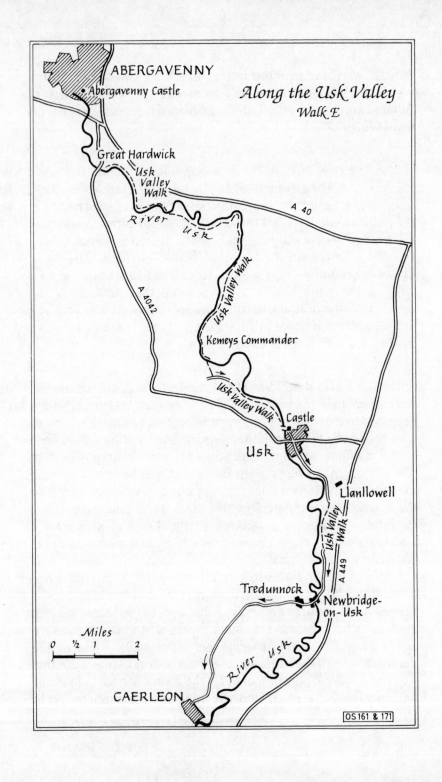

ABERGAVENNY

• Abergavenny Castle

Along the Usk Valley
Walk E

Great Hardwick

Usk Valley Walk

A 40

River Usk

A 40A2

Usk Valley Walk

Kemeys Commander

Usk Valley Walk

Castle

Usk

Llanllowell

Usk Valley Walk

A 449

Tredunnock

Newbridge-on-Usk

Miles

0 ½ 1 2

River Usk

CAERLEON

OS 161 & 171

enhanced by the cackling of the geese who wander among the stones, flowers and hedges.

The twelfth-century keep overlooks the bowl of the hills in which modern Usk has been built over the place where 10,000 men of the twentieth legion had their barracks from 55–65 AD. However, it would not have been from there, but from the Benedictine Priory Church of St Mary in the centre of the old market town that Baldwin and William Saltmarsh preached the cross, and to Gerald's uncharacteristically naive astonishment, recruited some of the most notorious criminals in the district. He must surely have known that by volunteering their services for a holy war, these ruffians gained an automatic pardon for their misdeeds. So it was no wonder that Usk prison emptied. It was a chance worth taking, for who could say whether the expedition to the Holy Land would ever take place, whereas the immediate laws of retribution were otherwise inescapable.

The Usk Valley Walk continues to the south of the town, from the village of Llanllowell, and follows the east bank of the river to the crossing at Newbridge-on-Usk, where it joins the main road to Caerleon, which runs above the flood-plain to the west, a sea of red, swirling mud in heavy weather. The lane from Newbridge passes through the hamlet of Tredunnock then on to Caerleon. The church at Tredunnock holds an inscribed Roman stone so placed that it is the first thing to strike the attention of anyone entering the building. Someone has kindly provided an English translation of the Latin, so that all may know what was in the mind of the lady who set the memorial up. 'To the Gods below' it reads, 'Julius Julianus, a soldier of the second legion, the Augustina, of 18 years service and 40 years of age has been buried here at the charge of his beloved wife.'

Julius Julianus must have been stationed in Caerleon, whose   *Caerleon*
name as Gerald tells us means 'the city of Legions, Caer, in the British language signifying a city or camp, for there the Roman legions, sent into this island, were accustomed to winter'.

He was as delighted with the place as any modern visitor must be, and found it:

of undoubted antiquity, and handsomely built of masonry, with courses of bricks, by the Romans. Many vestiges of its former splendour may yet be seen; immense palaces, formerly ornamented with gilded roofs, in imitation of Roman magnificence, in as much as they were first raised by the Roman princes, and embellished with splendid buildings; a tower of prodigious size, remarkable hot baths, relics of temples, and theatres, all enclosed within fine walls, parts of which remain standing. You will find on all sides, both within and without the circuit of the walls, subterraneous buildings, aquaducts, underground passages; and what I think worthy of notice, stoves contrived with wonderful art, to transmit the heat insensibly through narrow tubes passing up the side walls.

When he came here with Baldwin, Gerald had not yet visited Rome. Yet he seems to have been well able to interpret the antiquities of Caerleon, which the Romans knew as Isca. The surprising thing is that it took the latter-day archaeologists so long to puzzle out the workings of the hypercaust system here, which remained a mystery to them until 1964, although Gerald was able to describe it so precisely. Admittedly there was much more of Roman Isca left for Gerald to speculate on. The heavily roofed buildings were in use as barns from the fourth century, and they were not to be fully demolished until the thirteenth, at which time they became quarries of other buildings.

Now, a walk round the substantial remains of the amphitheatre and the barracks, and a visit to the splendidly laid-out excavated area of the baths and to the newly-opened Roman legionary museum, induces an acute awareness of the patterned web of time. Eight hundred years lie between our day and Gerald's, almost exactly the same interval which stretched between his time and the departure of the legions from Isca. Yet there is a strong feeling that, in many ways, Rome is much closer to modern life than the British middle ages.

This feeling is reflected in the paradox which a modern reader must discern in Gerald's view of the world. He was able to describe the distant past with a formal precision, yet at the same time he took a delight in retelling the most outrageous fantasies of folk-lore, in the same matter-of-fact tone that he uses to write of Roman bricks.

Caerleon put him in mind of two such stories. The first relates to a prophecy of the Merlin of Arthurian romance, a figure by whom he was continually fascinated. Although as a general rule he had little time for his fellow writer Geoffrey of Monmouth (as the next story makes clear), he unashamedly followed his work when he wanted to consider Caerleon as Arthur's Camelot; a tradition that persisted to the Victorian age. It was here, at the Hanbury Arms, by the main bridge over the Usk, that Tennyson came to write *The Idylls of the King*. For Gerald, Caerleon was the place where Roman ambassadors received audience at King Arthur's Court, but his main concern was to draw attention to Merlin's prophecy, quoted by Geoffrey, that the Christian metro-politan see would eventually be moved from Caerleon to St David's settlement at Menevia. No doubt he was happy to remind Baldwin of this, and to have the chance of doing so in the presence of the Bishops of Llandaff and St David's, as the entourage rode through Caerleon on its way to Newport.

The prophecies of Merlin reminded him of the bard Meilyr, who lived in Caerleon until his death in 1137. This man had 'an extraordinary familiarity with unclean spirits, by seeing them, knowing them, talking with them, and calling each by his proper name, he was enabled, through their assistance, to foretell future events'. These spirits gave him the power to discern a lie and 'if he looked on a book, faultily or falsely written, or containing a false passage, although wholly illiterate, he would point out the place with his finger'. With some ingratitude Gerald recounts that although the evil spirits left Meilyr in peace whenever he held St John's Gospel, if ever Geoffrey of Monmouth's works were put in his hands 'they instantly reappeared in greater numbers, and remained a longer time than usual on his body and on the book'.

Gerald says nothing of Meilyr's verse, but perhaps some of it was to come to his mind later in the course of his journey, for when he was in North Wales he wrote of the holy island of Bardsey, where the poet longed to be buried. However before Gerald reached that northern peninsular, he had to contend with the journey to Llandaff, and the treacherous quicksands of the southern coast.

CHAPTER FOUR

Along the South Coast

Despite Gerald's clear delight in the place, Baldwin and his accompanying bishops did not tarry in Caerleon, but rode through it, as they had to in order to cross the Usk once again and make their way to Newport, where Gerald tells us that 'many persons were induced to take the cross'. The preaching cross, from which the Archbishop exhorted the people, now stands in the grounds of St Woolos, which has been a cathedral since 1921, but although there has probably been a church on this site since the sixth century, that cross was not erected here. Local historians have good reason to believe that it originally stood a little further west, where Stow Hill meets Havelock Street, a high vantage point from which John Wesley preached on a number of occasions. It was here that a missing part of the ancient cross was discovered.

When Baldwin came to Stow Hill, it was crowned by a motte and bailey castle, destroyed when the railway tunnel was excavated in 1840. The Norman, Robert FitzHamon, who put that building in place was also responsible for erecting on the sixth-century site a new church, much of whose fabric still remains. Gerald must have observed the columns, carved with classical designs, which were brought from pagan Caerleon to adorn the west doorway of the Christian church.

Those columns are there, but much has been lost, for St Woolos has been twice restored since the mid-nineteenth century. Now, as a cathedral, it dominates an industrial city which has grown up on the site of the sixth-century settlement, which clustered round the hill on which it stands. Legend has it that the Celtic chieftain, Gwynllyw, was inspired by a dream to set up his headquarters at a place where he was to find a white ox

Newport and St Woolos

with a black spot on its forehead. So he journeyed through Gwent until he came to this hill above the Usk, where he discovered such an animal grazing. There he encamped and by some unrelated means was immediately converted to Christianity by his son, the saintly Cadoc, who had presumably already settled his llan in this place. From that time on, Gwynllyw's own life became so devout that it was thought right to dedicate the church to him, and to give his name, somewhat Anglicised to Woolos, to the surrounding Wentlooge levels which lie between the city and the Severn Sea.

Wentlooge

Baldwin's entourage splashed its way to Cardiff across this morass. After centuries of draining, the flatlands recall the dairy pastures of the Somerset wetlands and the horticultural acres of the Fens. But Wentlooge levels are wilder than both those places, the areas of dry ground are much smaller, and more horses than cattle graze the rough grass. Nevertheless the place once had a reputation for being particularly salubrious for humans and earlier in this century it was quite the custom for Newport families to send their children who had been suffering from such ailments as whooping cough to convalesce by this inland sea.

Despite the careful, systematic drainage, which may even have been started by the Romans, these levels have often been subject to floods, such as the fearful inundation of 1606 commemorated in St Brides church. Even now anybody travelling here in wet and windy weather has to be careful not to land up in one of the reed-edged reens spilling across the dividing lane.

Walk A: Across the levels to Cardiff (OS sheet 171)

A walk across Wentlooge starts from Newport's Tredegar House Country Park to the south-west of the city, where the Morgans, the lords of Tredegar, made their home from 1402 until 1951, when the house was taken over by a school which ran for twenty-three years, after which Newport Borough Council bought it, restoring the building to some of the glory of its heyday and

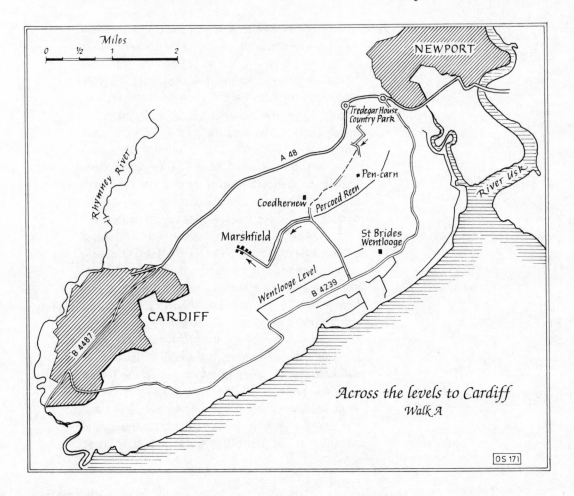

Across the levels to Cardiff
Walk A

OS 171

opening it to the public. From the woodland walk by the lake in
these grounds, a lane runs south towards the farm of Pen-carn
and passes the footpath which leads south-west to Coedkernew.

The farm of Pen-carn stands on slightly higher ground above
the reen of Percoed, where an old road ran across the marshes
which could only be reached by a long-disused ford, concerning
which Merlin Sylvester had a prophecy to make, that Gerald
could not forbear to quote:

'Whenever you shall see a mighty prince with a freckled face make an hostile irruption into the southern part of Britain, should he cross the ford of Pen-carn, then know ye that the force of Cambria shall be brought low.' Now it came to pass in our times, that Henry II took up arms against Rhys, the son of Gruffydd, and directed his march through the southern part of Wales towards Caermardyn. On the day that he intended to pass over Nant Pen-carn, the old Britons of the neighbourhood watched his approach towards the ford with the utmost solicitude; knowing, since he was both mighty and freckled, that if the passage of the destined ford was accomplished, the prophecy concerning him would undoubtedly be fulfilled. When the king had followed the road leading to a more modern ford of the river (the old one spoken of in the prophecy having been for a long time in disuse), and was preparing to pass over, the pipers and trumpeters . . . began to sound their instruments on the opposite bank, in honour of the king. The king's horse, startling at the wild, unusual noise, refused to obey the spur and enter the water; upon which the king, gathering up the reins, hastened in violent wrath to the ancient ford, which he rapidly passed; and the Britons returned to their homes, alarmed and dismayed at the destruction which seemed to await them.

It so happened that the prophecy was in a sense fulfilled. In the winter of 1161, Lord Rhys was forced to surrender to the English King at Pencader, to the north of Carmarthen, although he saved his nation's honour by loudly declaring in Welsh for the benefit of his followers that the Cymri would never be defeated. Moreover he swore that on the Day of Judgement no other nation or language would answer for his people.

Cardiff Castle   Baldwin had to cross the Rhymney River in order to reach Cardiff, and must have been well aware of doing so, but nowadays the motorist driving east from Marshfield into the gleaming, white city centre follows such a network of roads that the river crossing is obscured. The civic and university buildings of Cardiff stand squarely beside the ruins of the castle where Baldwin spent the night. Gerald writes about the events of 1158, when William, Earl of Gloucester, who held the castle at that time, was abducted with his wife and small son by a Welshman whose land he was trying to snatch. At that time, according to Gerald, 'the castle of Caerdyf was surrounded with high walls, guarded by one hundred and twenty men-at-arms, a numerous body of archers, and a strong watch.' These walls, which the intrepid Welshman scaled, had been set up by Robert FitzHamon soon after the Conquest on the site of a Roman fort, built in the fourth century as a defence from sea attacks. FitzHamon's enclosure now embraces a nineteenth-century castellated building which houses the Royal Welch, a regiment which has notable battle honours to its credit, and which must relish Gerald's praise of Welsh bravery when he commended men who 'anxiously study the defence of their country and their liberty; for these they fight, for these they undergo hardships, and for these willingly sacrifice their lives'.

FitzHamon threw up a high motte in the north-west corner of the Roman fort; and it was in the high, white stone keep on the top of this moated earthwork that Baldwin rested before crossing the Taff, Cardiff's other river, in order to reach the cathedral of Llandaff. Although it is still possible to climb the steps to that white tower, St Piran's chapel, the other building which Gerald connected with Cardiff, has disappeared. He tells us that it was at that church that Henry II was taken sadly to task for permitting Sunday trading. The king, who had just returned from Ireland was leaving the building after hearing Mass, when

> a man of fair complexion, with a round tonsure and meagre countenance, tall and about forty years of age, habited in a white robe falling down to his naked feet, thus addressed him in the Teutonic tongue: 'God hold thee, cuing,' which signifies, 'May God protect you,

king'; and proceeded in the same language, 'Christ and his Holy Mother, John the Baptist, and the Apostle Peter salute thee, and command thee strictly to prohibit throughout thy whole dominion every kind of buying or selling on Sundays, and not to suffer any work to be done on those days, except such as relates to the preparation of daily food; that due attention may be paid to the performance of the divine offices. If thou dost this, all thy undertakings shall be successful, and thou shalt lead a happy life.' The king, in French, desired Philip de Mecros, who held the reins of his horse, to ask the rustic if he had dreamt this, and when the soldier explained to him the king's question in English, he replied in the same language he had before used, 'Whether I have dreamt it or not, observe what day this is,' (addressing himself to the king, not to the interpreter), 'and unless thou shalt do so, and quickly amend thy life, before the expiration of one year, thou shalt hear such things concerning what thou lovest best in this world, and shalt thereby be so much troubled, that thy disquietude shall continue to thy life's end.'

The king's immediate reaction was to dig his spurs into his horse, then on second thoughts, he decided to talk again to the prophetic rustic, but he was too late. The man had vanished. However his predictions came true. The following year the king's three avaricious and quarrelsome sons deserted their father's forces and swore allegiance to Louis of France. So perhaps, in 1987 our rulers were wise to acquiesce in parliament's pious rejection of the bill that would have allowed Sunday trading to take place again, 800 years later.

Llandaff

In Llandaff, Baldwin escorted by Peter de Leia, and Llandaff's Bishop Saltmarsh, spoke to the people, who had gathered on the green above the hollow in which the cathedral lies, hidden from seaborne invaders. Here, where a ruined bell tower now frames the cathedral spire, the English stood together on one side, the Welsh on the other and, as Gerald records, 'many persons of each nation took the cross'. As far as the Welsh were concerned, that must have been due to the services of Archdeacon Alexander of Bangor who made Baldwin's words intelligible to them.

That night Baldwin slept in the bishop's palace as the guest of William Saltmarsh, whom Gerald knew as a 'discreet and good man'. Only three years before, when Saltmarsh had been abbot of St Augustine's in Bristol, Baldwin himself had consecrated him to the bishopric of Llandaff. Saltmarsh was to die in 1191, and immediately the bishopric was offered to Gerald, who refused it out of hand, for his sights were firmly set on St David's. It is ironic that when the Church of Wales finally became independent of Canterbury the archbishopric that Gerald longed to restore went to Llandaff and not to St David's.

Llandaff Cathedral

In 1402, Saltmarsh's palace was completely destroyed during the rebellion of Owen Glendower, and entrance to the present choir school is made through the ruins of a later building. Nor is there much left of the cathedral in which Baldwin celebrated Mass the following morning, for the rebuilding of the original church here which started in 1120 according to plans laid down by Urban, Llandaff's first Norman bishop, went on almost continually until the present day. However Gerald could still recognise the fine and elaborately carved Norman chancel arch, and the doorway, which leads into the regimental chapel of the Royal Welch.

Now the interior of the cathedral is dominated by Epstein's majestic Christ, mounted on a gold-encrusted cylinder and supported by a concrete arch that spans the nave. Many people find its impact on an ancient building both unsettling and incongruous, but Gerald would probably have accepted it happily enough, living as he did in a time of rapid innovation in church architecture and one in which the brilliant colours with which the internal plaster and woodwork were painted would seem almost blasphemously garish to modern eyes.

Barry Island

In fact the interior of a twelfth-century church could well put one in mind of the sort of holiday camp now flourishing on Barry Island, which Gerald passed by with a nod of family pride as the Archbishop rode west. For his Norman father, William de Barri, took his name from this rock, protruding into the Bristol Channel, on which the sixth-century hermit, Baruc, lived and died. It is no place for a hermitage now, though it might have served as such in the sixteenth century when Leland was able to describe it as an island which was 'about a mile in cumpace, and hath very good corne, grasse, and sum wood; the ferme of it worth a £10 a yere. There ys no dwelling in the isle, but there is in the middle of it a fair little chapel of St Barrok, where much pilgrimage was usid'. By the time Sir Richard Colt Hoare came to translate Gerald's work in 1806, the chapel had disappeared and a great dock had connected the island 'now covered with houses' to the mainland.

St Illtud's College (OS sheet 170)

William Saltmarsh accompanied Baldwin to the edge of his diocese, but seems not to have insisted that the Archbishop should visit its most holy place, St Illtud's settlement at Llaniltud Fawr (now oddly Englished to Llantwit Major) for many years one of the most important settlements of the Celtic church. The college that St Illtud founded here was attended by St Samson, who was later to become bishop of Dol in Brittany. The present church, like the cathedral of Llandaff, is set in a hollow to hide it from invading pirates, for the lush pastures of this coastal plane attracted many land-hungry peoples long before the Normans started to push west. Danes, Vikings, Irish, and even in 1050 a raiding party of Saxons from the summer lands across the water, all made landings here.

St Illtud's is now really two churches standing end to end. The most westerly, built about 1100, serves as a sort of museum of Celtic crosses of the eighth and ninth centuries, which stand under a roof of timeless bog oak. Here is the cross of St Illtud himself, inscribed with his name and a Latin text informing us that Samson caused it to be erected. That saint also raised a seven-foot pillar for the repose of his own soul and for those of two contemporary kings in the region.

Baldwin's cavalcade did not journey so far south. They were bound for the priory cell of Ewenny to the east of the River Ogmore. To reach it, they probably followed the Roman road (now covered by the A 48) and so went westwards along the way which the drovers of the seventeenth century would have used to bring their cattle east through the town of Cowbridge. It is, however, much pleasanter to take the coastal lane from Llantwit Major, through St Donats and Marcross, home of that Philip who acted as Henry II's interpreter outside St Piran's chapel in Cardiff.

Walk B: To Ewenny Priory

This lane runs through gentle farming country. A couple of miles to the south-east of St Brides Major, a path goes to the coastal parkland of Dunraven, from where it is possible to walk west across wide sheep-grazed downs sloping towards the natural rock pavements of the shore. In early autumn the grass here gleams with golden gorse and the scarlet berries of wild arum.

On the outskirts of the town of Ogmore-by-Sea a footpath heads inland towards the upper reaches of the River Ogmore, where it is joined by the Ewenny. The ruins of Ogmore Castle, originally built to defend an easy crossing of the river, stand at the bank here. On this side the land is firm enough, but anyone venturing across the stepping stones that now span the water, will enter a fluctuating landscape composed of the high sand-dunes that make up so much of the Welsh coastline. They are often a delight to walk through now, but Baldwin's horses were to find them treacherous and difficult to the point of near-disaster.

Ewenny Priory was built further up-river. It was founded in 1141 by Maurice de Londres, Lord of Ogmore Castle, who gave it as a daughter house to the Benedictine Abbey at Gloucester. He chose that it should stand in the land to the west of St Michael's church, which his father, William, had established and which was to become the priory church.

The battlemented ruins of the Norman priory at Ewenny are a reminder that its cell was soon to become a fortified monastery,

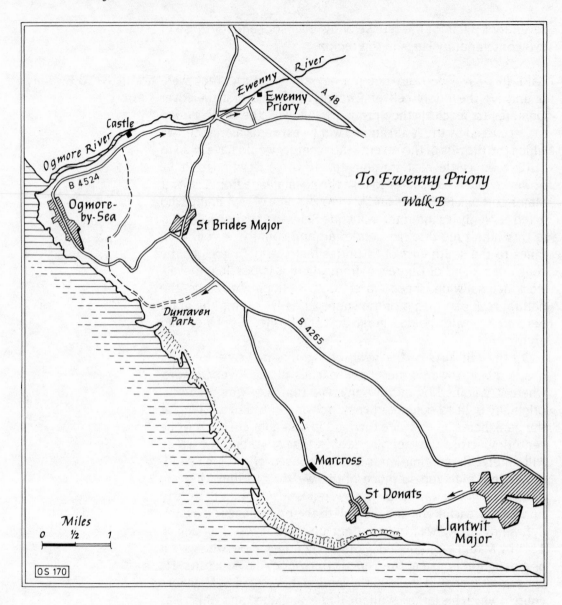

Ogmore River

Castle

B 4524

Ogmore-by-Sea

Ewenny River

Ewenny Priory

A 48

To Ewenny Priory
Walk B

St Brides Major

Dynraven Park

B 4265

Marcross

St Donats

Llantwit Major

Miles
0   ½   1

OS 170

constantly under threat of attack by the Welsh. Most of the five
acres that its walls enclosed are in private hands, which means
that there is only restricted access to these ruins. Nor is it always

easy to get inside the parish church of St Michael's, whose east end, which inspired one of Turner's paintings, is all that now remains of William de Londres' building. Just past the church a footbridge crosses the narrow river whose banks support an invasion of Himalayan balsam, a plant that would have astonished medieval eyes almost as much as the heavy traffic running along the A 48 from here to Margam.

It was to Margam that Baldwin went next, riding to the abbey, which stood in undulating, wooded country, an inland area, which now serves as a country park for Bridgend, Neath and Port Talbot. Gerald was unstinting in his praise for this 'noble Cistercian monastery' which had been founded forty years previously. He commended its abbot, Conan, for his good sense and learning and was pleased to recount an episode to prove the generosity of an abbey which was

Margam Abbey

more celebrated for its charitable deeds than any other of that order in Wales . . . As a reward for that abundant charity which the monastery had always, in times of need, exercised towards strangers and poor persons, in a season of approaching famine, their corn and provisions were perceptibly, by divine assistance, increased, like the widow's cruse of oil . . . In our own time too, in a period of scarcity, while great multitudes of poor were daily crowding before the gates for relief, by the unanimous consent of the brethren, a ship was sent to Bristol to purchase corn for charitable purposes. The vessel delayed by contrary winds, and not returning (but rather affording an opportunity for the miracle), on the very day when there would have been a total deficiency of corn, both for the poor and for the convent, a field near the monastery was found suddenly to ripen, more than a month before the usual time of harvest: thus divine Providence supplied the brotherhood and the numerous poor with sufficient nourishment until autumn.

Margam's tradition for hospitality is unabated, although nowadays the nourishment it provides comes in the form of art. During the annual summer exhibitions held in this parkland, the generous open spaces are adorned with sculpture by artists of such international renown as Barbara Hepworth and Anthony Caro. They provide a pleasing counterpoint to the collection of early Christian stones, discovered among the earthworks of the hill-fort on Mynydd Margam and now displayed in the old school house attached to the parish church. That church still bears many traces of its Norman origin, although it was substantially restored in the nineteenth century.

At the dissolution, the lands of Margam Abbey passed to the Talbots, a family which laid out their grounds in the best eighteenth-century parkland fashion, building an immense orangery, said to be the largest in the world. It is now used as an exhibition gallery and concert hall.

Gerald's high praise for Margam arose partly from his prejudice in favour of the Cistercians, an austere, hard-working order, and one which, unlike the Benedictines, allowed Welshmen to enter their institutions and take their vows. Neath Abbey, whose ruins stand in the industrial estate to the north-west of Margam, was another Cistercian foundation. Baldwin, however, did not visit it. Instead, he hoped to hurry on his journey by daring the quicksands that lay round the southern shore. That choice of route had fearsome results, for having forded the river Afan, the Archbishop and his companions

proceeded along the sea-shore towards the river Neth, which, on account of its quicksands, is the most dangerous and inaccessible river in South Wales. A pack-horse belonging to the author, which had proceeded by the lower way near the sea, although in the midst of many others, was the only one which sunk down into the abyss, but he was at last, with great difficulty, extricated, and not without some damage done to the baggage and books. Yet although we had Morgan, the prince of that country, as our conductor,

*we did not reach the river without great peril, and some
severe falls: for the alarm occasioned by this unusual
kind of road, made us hasten our steps over the
quicksands, in opposition to the advice of our guide, and
fear quickened our pace; whereas, through these difficult
passages, as we there learned, the mode of proceeding
should be made with moderate speed.*

After that experience, it was no wonder that they did not
attempt to ford the Neath, but took a boat over the water,
presumably getting the wretched horses to swim across. Colt
Hoare suggested that this river crossing was made from Briton
Ferry, at the place where the A 483 goes by Neath docks now. If
so, it was at that place that Baldwin bade farewell to William
Saltmarsh, who had accompanied the Archbishop to the bound-
ary of his diocese of Llandaff. The country to the west of the river
belonged to St David's, whose bishop, Peter de Leia, had not left
Baldwin's side since he set out from Hereford.

*Across the Neath to
Swansea (OS sheet
159)*

Relieved at having such a difficult part of their journey behind
them, the Archbishop's entourage stayed for a couple of nights in
Swansea castle, a building which has now disappeared. As
Swansea grew, it became surrounded by houses. As the centuries
passed, the old fortification served its time as a prison, and then
after many more substantial modifications as the offices of the
Cambrian Daily Leader. Not much of the Norman fortification was
left by then, and all that is left to us now is a print of 1741
showing the wooded motte which supported the keep where
Baldwin slept. The ruins of a so-called castle in the centre of
Swansea do not mark the place; they are the remains of an early
fourteenth-century fortified manor house.

Gerald knew this port both by its Welsh name of Abertawe and
as Sweynsei, that is Sweyne's island, named for the ninth-century
Viking, Sweyn Forkbeard, son of Harold Bluetooth of Denmark,
who settled here and dominated most of the lands of Gower. No
doubt Gerald gave the assembled company the benefit of his
reflection on the Danes as the Archbishop and his companions
relaxed before starting off on the next stage of their journey.

Certainly he thought it worthwhile to digress from his own strenuous outline of the itinerary and to quote two light-hearted monks discussing the dangers of the journey. 'One of them said (alluding to the wildness of the country), "This is a hard province." The other (alluding to the quicksands), wittily replied, "Yet yesterday it was found too soft." '

Possibly Baldwin and Peter de Leia were more entertained by a long fairy story, which Gerald also interjects at this point. It was appropriate enough, for he avers that it was a tale told to his uncle, when he was bishop of St David's, by an old man, who confessed that as a youth of twelve, when he was already training for the priesthood, he had wandered into an enchanted land. It happened when he ran away from school 'in order to avoid the discipline and frequent stripes inflicted on him by his preceptor'. For two days, he hid in a hollow bank, then when hunger was about to drive him back to his teachers, two diminutive men appeared, who led the lad into the most beautiful country 'adorned with rivers and meadows, woods and plains'. Here he was introduced to the king, and entered into a Utopia, where the people

> *neither ate flesh nor fish, but lived on milk diet, made up into messes with saffron. They never took an oath, for they detested nothing so much as lies. As often as they returned from our upper hemisphere, they reprobated our ambition, infidelities, and inconstancies; they had no form of public worship, being strict lovers and reverers, as it seemed, of truth.*

The boy, too, was able to return to his own world in order to visit his mother, who immediately became greedy for the rich delights that her son was enjoying and begged him to bring her a present of one of the golden objects with which the fairy-land abounded. So he stole a golden ball, while he was playing with the king's son 'and brought it to his mother in great haste; and when he reached the door of his father's house, but not unpursued, and was entering it in a great hurry, his foot stumbled on the threshold, and falling down into the room where his mother was sitting, the two pigmies seized the ball which had dropped from his hand, and departed, shewing the boy every mark of contempt and derision'.

Thereafter the lad was totally unable to find his way back to the fairy country, although the memory of the enchanted land never faded.

That sounds very like one of the tales of the Tylwyth Tag (the fairy people of the peninsula of Gower), which may be why Gerald chose to insert it into his narrative at this stage of his journey. For although Baldwin went straight on from Swansea to the west, without making a detour to the enchanted peninsula, there are good reasons for thinking that Gerald's familiarity with it went well beyond his obvious delight in the fairy story that must surely have issued from this magical strip of land.

He was well aware that the holy Caradoc, who died in 1124, spent part of his life as a hermit here, living as a solitary at the shrine of the sixth-century Cenydd of Llangennith. Perhaps it was because Caradoc was reputed to have been born at Brecon, that Gerald took such an intense interest in the reputation of that holy man; but whatever the cause, he made strenuous but unsuccessful attempts to persuade Innocent III to have him canonised. As Gerald was so thorough in everything that he undertook, it seems most probable that he would have made his own pilgrimages to the places associated with the early-twelfth-century priest, whose cause he advocated so strenuously.

In any case, by the twelfth century, Gower was a perennial place of pilgrimage, and it would have been so even if Caradoc had never ventured there. For the sixth-century Cenydd, whom Caradoc venerated, drew countless pilgrims to his shrine, seeking the healing powers of his relics. Cenydd is traditionally held to be the son of Gildas, first historian of Britain; but many strange legends sprang up about this holy Welshman, who, like many of his priestly contemporaries, finally settled in Brittany where his cult became established at Ploumelin. That may well have given rise to the tale that he was actually Breton in origin, having been born of an incestuous union between a prince of that country and his beautiful daughter. The story goes that the birth occurred when King Arthur was holding court in Gower, and that as a stigma of the baby's unnatural conception he came into the world with one leg permanently doubled up to his thigh.

Desperate to hide this evidence of his son's deformity, his father ordered that the child should be cast into the waters of the Loughor as it flowed to the north of the peninsula. As the baby tossed on the waves, seagulls came to its rescue, carrying the child up into the air and depositing him gently on the high-tide island of Worms Head, where he was miraculously fed by the divine gift of a breast-shaped bell, which provided the infant with all the nourishment that he needed. However, it was not Worms Head but Burry Holms, the high-tide island on the opposite extremity of the peninsula, which was the goal of thousands of pilgrims, who came across the sand dunes here in order to reach the chapel commemorating the solitary hermitage of the adult Cenydd.

**Walk C:
Llangennith and
Rhossili**

Today, a Cenydd pilgrimage must start from his church at Llangennith, founded on the site where the saint made his first settlement, after he left Illtud's college at Llantwit Major. The church that his monks built there was destroyed in a Viking invasion of 986, but the saint's grave slab still remains, a stone carved with interlacing patterns set into the west wall of the nave of a much-restored twelfth-century church. Here too a modern carving is displayed, reminding visitors of the fable that grew up around the deformed saint, who is said to have relished his stigma and refused healing at the hands of St David himself.

From Llangennith, a lane leads to Broughton Burrows, a place whose wealth of flowers provides pilgrimage enough. Here is an enchantment woven out of a luxuriant purple mist formed by banks of low-growing thyme interspersed with the brilliantly shining pink of convolvulus, pyramid orchids and century; the deep red of bloody cranesbill, the muted tones of the silver sea-thistle and the pale rose flush of yarrow.

This part of the journey needs careful timing. Anyone who is held for too long by the spell of the flowers may miss the tide and

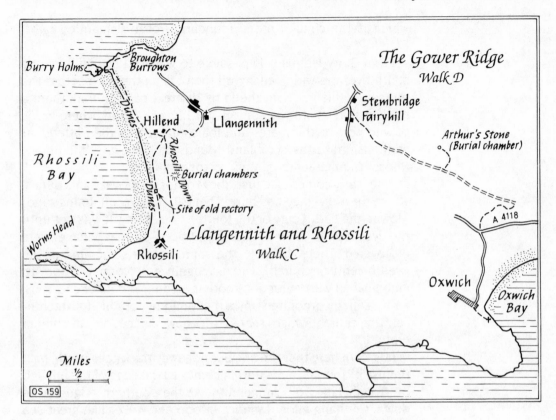

The Gower Ridge
Walk D

Arthur's Stone
o (Burial chamber)

Stembridge
Fairyhill

Burry Holms
Broughton
Burrows

Dunes

Hillend
Llangennith

Rhossili
Bay

Rhossili Down

Burial chambers

Dunes

Site of old rectory

Worms Head

Llangennith and Rhossili
Walk C

Rhossili

A 4118

Oxwich

Oxwich
Bay

Miles
0   ½   1

OS 159

have to wait several hours before it becomes possible to walk across to Burry Holms. Even then, the sands uncovered by the tides are soft enough in patches to give the walker an uneasy understanding of the quicksands of Neath that so nearly engulfed Gerald's packhorse.

The island is well worth that moment's uneasiness. There are two ruins on its eastern extremity, but they are so vestigial that it is not easy to decide which one represents the Celtic hermit's cell, and which is the medieval pilgrims' chapel or hostel. There can be no confusion, however, about the more distant past and a remnant of recent years, for at the western end of the island, a deep ditch marks the outer defences of an iron-age fort, beyond which is the circular stone foundation of a dismantled light-house.

From Burry Holms it is possible to walk to Rhossili by going south over the wide beach and then taking the path across the dunes to Hillend. From the fairly discreet caravan park there a track goes beneath the contours of Rhossili Down, where herds of wild ponies, the mares and foals guarded by their attendant stallions, graze the scrubland round the low white building of Rhossili's nineteenth-century rectory.

That path comes out just above Rhossili's own sand dunes, where the old village was buried beneath an overwhelming sand-blow in the early years of the fourteenth century. It was not until the wet winter of 1979–80 that traces of that village were discovered. There, deep in the sand were the remains of the twelfth-century church, whose magnificent Norman doorway, embellished with outer dog-tooth moulding and inner chevrons, had been incorporated into the building of the fourteenth-century church which served the new village on the higher ground.

It is from here that the ancient ridgeway track goes north, past prehistoric burial cairns until it comes to the edge of the hill and the rough lanes of Llangennith. At the southern edge of the down, the hang-glider fanatics swoop and hover like great sea birds over Rhossili Bay. Away beyond them lies the island of Lundy and further still the outline of the north Devon coast, both of which are clearly visible in good weather.

Walk D: The Gower Ridge

On such a day, it is also well worthwhile to walk the main ridge of Gower and look out over the whole extent of the fairy kingdom of Gerald's story. It is a walk that starts from the appropriately named Fairyhill, although the origin of that name is lost somewhere in the annals of the leading Gower family. They once owned the house that now has the name, but it currently serves as an hotel. The path from here climbs slowly through scrubby ground to the wide ridgeway path, from which streams flow northwards. This means that the ground to the left is treacher-ously marshy. However a wide, solid track goes safely across the bog-land to visit two bronze-age cairns, one of which has a massive split cap-stone, which has earned it the name of Arthur's stone.

Gower is indeed full of Arthurian stories, and that is another aspect of the place which would have endeared it to Gerald, who shared his generation's intense fascination with the legendary monarch. A path going south from the ridgeway leads down to Oxwich Bay and the woods that almost hide its tiny thirteenth-century church, dedicated to St Illtud. It is said that when the sixth-century saint came to seek a time of solitary prayer in the caves of this shore, a corpse was brought to him, and believing that it was probably the body of Arthur, he caused a church to be built over it. The present church is meant to stand on that site.

Gerald, who was to support the monks of Glastonbury when they claimed that the king was buried in their abbey, must have renounced that story. In 1188 however, his mind was no doubt on more immediate matters as he rode out of Swansea with Baldwin towards Kidwelly and the Loughor river, which they undoubtedly crossed by boat, at the place where road and rail now go over the water. A ferry still ran from here in Colt Hoare's time.

Two lesser rivers lay before the Archbishop on his journey north-west, both of which flowed into the Gwendraeth estuary, whose Welsh name translates as white sands. The Gwendraeth Fawr is still crossed by the ancient bridge of Pont Spwdwr, and it must have been at this place that the cavalcade crossed the river, going inland in order to avoid the marshes of the estuary. A more formidable crossing was to be made at the second Gwendraeth river, known as Gwendraeth Fach (ie the small one, although in fact it must have been much wider than its twin).

In the twelfth century large ships could be moored beneath the impressive banks that still support the massive walls of Kidwelly castle, which now tower above a rather muddy stream. Kidwelly's long industrial history has now all but vanished too; it is commemorated in the town museum and in the red-brick remains of the eighteenth-century tin-plate works which can be found up-stream from the castle.

Kidwelly

Baldwin reached that river-crossing to the castle by riding past the Benedictine priory, founded in 1130 as a cell of Sherborne Abbey. The Welsh priory church, whose spire was added to the tower in the thirteenth century still remains, but there is little to see of the actual castle in which Lord Rhys, who dominated the area at this time, offered the Archbishop the hospitality of a night's rest. Only the sheer earthworks supporting the present ruin, whose stones date from the late thirteenth century, are left to mark the place of the earlier fortification.

Some fifty years before Baldwin came here, Maurice de Londres, son of the founder of Ogmore and Ewenny, was lord of the timber-fortified earthwork on the banks of Gwendraeth Fach. The Welsh did not accept his domination easily, and in 1136, the Norman's castle was attacked by Gwenllian, Lord Rhys's Amazon mother, wife of Gruffydd ap Rhys, who had gone into North Wales to seek support for his southern wars. Her adventure ended tragically, for 'one of her sons who she had arrogantly brought with her in that expedition was slain, and the other, Malgo, taken prisoner; and she with many of her followers was put to death'.

She remains a town heroine still. Tradition has it that the farm of Maes Gwenllian (the field of Gwenllian) was built at the place where the lady died; and a school, a housing estate and an hotel in the modern town have all been given the name of the Welsh princess, who attacked a foreign stronghold.

Although Gwenllian could not get the better of de Londres, his own wife worsted him more successfully. Gerald obviously relished the story of the way she tricked him into reducing the herds of deer that roamed the extensive hunting forest that he had created on the hilly land, where the sheep grazed between the Gwendraeth Fach and the River Tywi. She resolutely declared that the stags were attacking the flocks, whose pasture had been turned into a hunting preserve, and 'to make her story more probable, she caused some wool to be inserted between the intestines of two stags which had been embowelled; and her husband thus artfully deceived, sacrificed his deer to the rapacity of his dogs.'

Baldwin had to traverse that forest in order to reach the Tywi estuary, where he was to cross the river and go north to Carmarthen, although nowadays the main road to that town goes east of the river from Kidwelly. Today, a narrow coastal lane indicates the way that the Archbishop went. It runs above the wide salt marshes and shifting sand dunes of the shore and below the inland hills, which provide just enough elevation to enable hang-gliders to become airborne. This lane leads to Ferryside, where boats still cross the wide estuary, as they did when Baldwin went over the water to Llanstephan, whose castle he kept to his left hand as he rode north along the west bank of the river.

CHAPTER FIVE

From the Tywi to St David's

Gerald does not specifically say that Lord Rhys rode with the Archbishop as he entered the heartland of the Welsh prince's domain on his journey along the west bank of the Tywi, but it seems reasonable enough to imagine that he did. Certainly Gerald takes pains to mention the castles of Llanstephan (which Baldwin rode close by) and of Laugharne (in Welsh, Talycharn) which lies well to the west of his route, both of which, as he records, Lord Rhys was to take by assault in the following year.

However, anyone travelling this way now, will be less concerned with the twelfth-century ravages of the Welsh prince, than with the reminder that this is Dylan Thomas country, for the place is permeated by his stories and poems. Beneath the thirteenth-century gateway of Llanstephan castle is the seaside holiday village, scene of the outing taken in A Visit to Grandpa, and further up-river at Llangain is the farm, immortalised as Fern Hill, the inspiration for one of Thomas's most quoted poems. That was the home of the poet's aunt, Ann Jones, whose nephew gave her a paradoxical epitaph, claiming that she needed 'no druid of her broken body'. She had one though, and not just in the starkly moving funeral poem that Thomas wrote for her; for she lived in the land of the arch-druid, Merlin, whose name is given to the stones of the burial mound above the farm.

Carmarthen

And moreover Gerald also says that Carmarthen itself 'signifies the city of Merlin, because, according to the British History, he was there said to have been begotten of an incubus'. That tradition is backed up by the story attached to the old tree stump, long preserved at the east end of Priory Street, because of the belief that the druid had prophesied, in appalling doggerel that 'when the oak shall tumble down, so will fall Carmarthen town'.

Yet Carmarthen, as Gerald really must have known, is much more likely to have got its name from Caer Maridunum, the Latinised Celtic name for the Roman fort, whose walls were still standing when Baldwin came here. At this place, the legions guarded the roads that intersected where the gently meandering Tywi flows through the most fertile valley in Wales. Henry I also found it necessary to defend this rich land, for he built a castle here, which, like that of Swansea, was to become the local gaol, before being finally cleared away to make room for municipal buildings. Nor is there anything to be seen of the Augustinian priory where Baldwin spent the night, but its fame lives on, for it was here that the *Black Book of Carmarthen*, the earliest extant manuscript in the Welsh language, was lovingly compiled.

In the twelfth century, the fertile valley of the Tywi was heavily wooded. Up-river from Carmarthen, where the rich farmlands have earned the wide water-meadows the name of Golden Grove, Lord Rhys had his main stronghold of Dynevor. It was after that Welsh prince had been forced to submit to Henry II at Pencader in 1163, that the king decided to have the resources and potential of this territory properly appraised so that he would know best how to divide the rich pickings among his Norman vassals. To this end, as Gerald tells us, he despatched a Breton knight, guided by Guaidanus, dean of that region, to

> *explore the situation of Dynevor castle, and the strength of the country. The priest, being desired to take the knight by the easiest and best road to the castle, led him purposely aside by the most difficult and inaccessible paths, and whenever they passed through woods, the priest, to the general surprise of all present, fed upon grass, asserting that, in time of need, the inhabitants of that country were accustomed to live upon herbs and roots. The knight returning to the king, and relating what had happened, affirmed that the country was uninhabitable, vile and inaccessible, and only affording*

food to a beastly nation, living like brutes. At length the
king released Rhys, having first bound him to fealty by
solemn oaths and the delivery of hostages.

Walk A: Dynevor
(OS sheet 159)

The princes of Deheubarth, the land of South Wales, guarded the wealth of this region from a chain of rocky strongholds, built above the river valley. Lord Rhys, himself, built the startling Carreg Cennen, up-river from Trapp on the slopes of the Black Mountain. It is now carefully preserved and manicured by CADW, a marked contrast to the ruins near Llandeilo, which stand on the site of the far more ancient stronghold of the princes of South Wales. This is Dynevor, where Rhodri the Great built a palace for his son Cadell in 876, on a site which Gerald describes as 'a lofty summit above the Tywi'. The ruined castle is not to be confused with the Dynevor Castle marked on the OS map, which is a much more recent, private dwelling and stands further back from the river. Indeed the course of the river has changed, for there is now a stretch of meadowland between the real Dynevor Castle's cliff and the river it once defended.

Today, it is a sleeping beauty of a castle, difficult to find and almost entirely hidden by tall woods and by the undergrowth and scrub that shroud its northern approach. It is best reached through the landscaped gardens set out around the iron-age fort above the town bridge. From here, woodland paths cleared by the West Wales Naturalist Trust, who own this stretch of land, lead past an old chapel (now used for the Trust's purposes) to the grey battlements of the cliff-top castle.

St Clears (OS sheet
158)

Although Gerald could not resist writing of the rich lands of Dynevor, and although Lord Rhys may well have gone there to look after his own affairs before preparing for the Archbishop's reception in his castle at Cardigan, Baldwin made no such detour. His route from Carmarthen went due west, through St Clears to the Cistercian abbey of Whitland. The track that he rode along is now covered by the A 40, which rushes traffic through

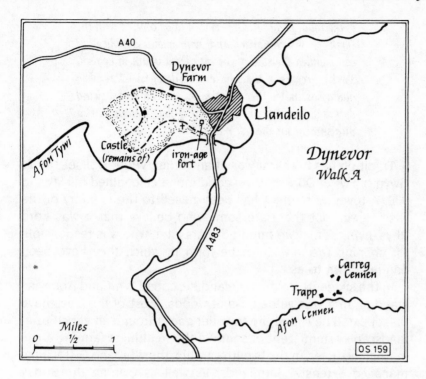

both these towns. Bound for the beautiful Pembrokeshire coast, few visitors pause in St Clears to look at the mound of its Norman castle, or the ornate twelfth-century chancel arch and font in the church that once served a small Cluniac priory, ruled from France and suppressed during the wars of Henry V.

Baldwin's next stop was at the Cistercians monastery of the **Whitland** White House beside the Taf, which gave its name to the present town. His journey there was not uneventful, for while he was on the road, he

> *was informed of the murder of a young Welshman, who*
> *was devoutly hastening to meet him; when turning out*

of the road, he ordered the corpse to be covered with the cloak of his almoner, and with pious supplication commended the soul of the murdered youth to heaven. Twelve archers of the adjacent castle of St Clare, who had assassinated the young man, were on the following day signed with the cross at Alba Domus, as a punishment for their crime.

Tradition has it, that it was at an earlier 'White House', the Ty Gwyn of Hywel Dda, that the good monarch codified his laws in 930. A town monument has been raised to the memory of the wise Hywel, but there are some who believe that it was Lord Rhys, living some two hundred years later, who was responsible for shaping the laws into the form in which they have been handed down to us.

In the sixteenth century, Leland described Whitland Abbey as standing in a vast wilderness of woods. Most of the trees have disappeared now, and the traveller goes through an agricultural landscape, reminiscent of some of the wealthiest farming areas in England. Even in the twelfth century, the Whitland Cistercians managed extensive farmlands, as well as owning the Friday fishing rights in the Viking-named town of Haverfordwest.

After the Danes came the Flemings, and Gerald reminds his readers that it was Henry I who first brought in people from the low countries to colonise these fat lands, which the Norman kings needed to secure for their nourishment and support. The Flemish settlement was to serve the turn of the English for centuries, so that Pembrokeshire eventually became a little England beyond Wales. It is a county which is still thought of as being divided east to west by the Landsker, a line formed by the ruins of a string of Norman castles, whose original purpose was to defend the rich lands of the south from the marauding Welsh of the rugged north. Below the line, where early vegetables for the London markets are now grown under wide expanses of plastic, the Englishry flourished. Above it, on the wild, hilly ground around St David's, the Welsh struggled to till unyielding soil.

Llawhaden is one of the most dramatic of the Norman castles of
the Landsker. It stands between Narberth and Haverfordwest on
the steep west bank of the Eastern Cleddau. By the twelfth
century it was serving its turn as a fortified stronghold for the
bishops of St David's. Gerald stayed here sometime in the mid
1170s, when he was about thirty, and his uncle held the
bishopric, which he was sure must eventually come to him. In
1192, Lord Rhys was to capture the castle as part of his bid to
extend his domain from Dynevor, but it was soon recovered for St
David's and by 1280, it was rebuilt on a magnificent scale as a
fortified mansion. Much of the present ruin dates from that time.

From Canaston Bridge, a footpath goes north to St Kenox, and
from there along the wooded river bank to the packhorse bridge
across the Eastern Cleddau, to the south of the superficially dull
church of St Aiddan, standing in an enchanting setting, surmounted by the fairy-tale towers of the forbidding, crag-perched
castle. From the church, a path goes through the woods to the
steep slope of the battlements. Inside the curtain walls, the place
seems gentle. The sheer rock is hidden, and the grass-covered
ring motte, which Lord Rhys demolished, is a flower-strewn
meadow, filled in spring and early summer with primroses,
cuckoo pint and spotted orchids.

Walk B: Llawhaden

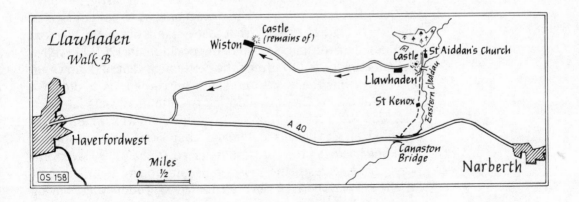

Haverfordwest   From here it is possible to go west, past the more fragmentary remains of another Landsker castle at Wiston, and so reach Haverfordwest where Baldwin and Gerald both preached to great effect there, so that although they addressed the people

> *in the Latin and French tongues, those persons who understood neither of those languages were equally affected, and flocked in great numbers to the cross. An old woman of those parts, who for three preceeding years had been blind, having heard of the archbishop's arrival, sent her son to the place where the sermon was to be preached, that he might bring back to her some particle, if only the fringe of his garment. The young man being prevented by the crowd from approaching the archbishop, waited till the assembly was dispersed, and then carried a piece of the earth on which the preacher had stood. The mother received the gift with great joy, and falling immediately on her knees, applied the turf to her mouth and eyes: and thus, through the merits of the holy man, and her own faith and devotion, recovered the blessing of sight, which she had entirely lost.*

Gerald does not say where that sermon was delivered, or whether the Archbishop stayed overnight in the priory, whose ruins now lie to the south of the town, or in the castle, in which, as Gerald writes, a prisoner had once managed to hold the son of the Earl of Clare to ransom. That castle stands above the Western Cleddau, in a virtually impregnable position. In 1205, Llewellyn the Great managed to ravage the settlement that had grown up around it, but the castle remained unscathed, as it did in a similar attack by Owen Glendower, two hundred years later.

It was eventually to succumb in the Civil War, when it was slighted at Cromwell's command; but some of the original building has been restored and replaced so that now Haverfordwest Castle serves as the county museum. The most striking part of the display here is devoted to Henry Tudor, who, having landed at Dale to the west of his birthplace in Pembroke castle, came here early in August 1485, on his way to defeat Richard III at Bosworth Field. With a Welsh monarch on the throne, the struggles between the Welsh and the English at last began to splutter out. The Tudors had no more loyal subjects than the Welsh folk, and the castles began to lose their threatening significance.

From Haverfordwest, Baldwin travelled directly to St David's, but before taking up the account of that journey, Gerald could not resist writing most lovingly of the region of his own birth and childhood, recounting episodes of its history and tradition. One such story concerns Caradoc, the hermit of Gower, whose canonisation Gerald advocated so strongly. At one stage in his life, this holy man sought another solitary retreat and found it, according to Gerald, at St Ishmael's, a place near enough to Haverfordwest for young Richard FitzTancred, son of the custodian of the castle, to visit him from time to time with gifts of food from his noble parents. It was the lad, himself, however, who 'so ingratiated himself in the eyes of the good man, that Caradoc very often promised him, together with his blessing, the portion of all his brothers, and the paternal inheritance.' It all came to pass, just as Caradoc said it would. Richard's older brothers all died before they could inherit. Gerald also tells of a visit which Richard made in which he was 'overtaken by a violent storm of rain, turned aside to the hermit's cell: and being unable to get his hounds near him, either by calling, coaxing, or by offering them food, the holy man smiled; and making a gentle motion with his hand, brought them all to him immediately.'

That story provides a pleasing rider to Gerald's many anecdotes of the thoughtless noblemen, who kenneled their hounds in churches, so bringing down upon themselves severe heaven-sent retribution for their blasphemy.

There is some confusion as to which St Ishmael's it was from which Caradoc made his prophetic pronouncement, and where he fondled his benefactor's hounds. Most writers on the region conclude that the incident occurred at Haroldston East, whose church is dedicated to St Ishmael. This is now a suburb of the ever-encroaching town of Haverfordwest, but in the early nineteenth century Colt Hoare was able to conclude that Caradoc's hermitage was 'probably near a place called Poorfield, the common on which Haverfordwest races are held, as there is a well there called Caradoc's Well, round which, till within these few years, there was a sort of vanity fair, where cakes were sold, and country games celebrated'.

There is a general denial of the suggestion that Caradoc might have spent his last solitary years at another St Ishmael's, lying to the west of Milford Haven. Yet it is not possible to discount this place entirely, for it is near the inlet where many of the pilgrims from Britanny, Devon and Cornwall landed on their way to St David's. And since the traditional role of hermits is to stand at a threshold and help travellers on their way, what could be more fitting than that the holy man should be there to greet them?

Walk C: St Ishmael's Church to the sea (OS sheet 157)

St Ishmael's church is a mile or so out of the holiday village that bears its name. It lies half hidden in the hollow of a wooded valley running to the sea, and from the position of old doorway arches and lintels, only two feet above the ground, it is clear that the present Victorian church supplants a much earlier building. Nor was that previous church by any means the first to stand here. The original one was founded in the sixth century by St Ishmael himself. Four hundred years later, the saint's Celtic cell became part of a teaching monastery, whose church was to be rebuilt by Caradoc.

The present building has to be kept locked and it is no easy matter to obtain the key. Those who do manage to get inside, however, will find a tenth-century cross, a remnant of a previous church and a stone which both Caradoc and Gerald must have venerated here. They would also have been familiar with the coastal inlet, although not so aware as a modern traveller must be of its peculiar delight and charm, for despite the holiday visitors and despite the close proximity of the industry of Milford Haven it remains remarkably peaceful, as anyone venturing through the woods to join the Pembrokeshire Coast Path as it runs to Musselwick Sands will find.

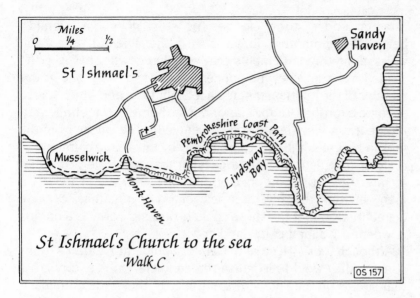

St Ishmael's Church to the sea
Walk C

The places that are more directly concerned with Gerald lie   *Carew Castle*
further to the south and east of the Pembroke river. Here is his
ancestral home of Carew castle, which his grandmother, the
Princess Nest brought as her marriage portion to his grandfather,
Gerald de Windsor, in 1100. As a young man, Gerald came here
with his uncle, the bishop of St David's, having promised succour
and support to some Flemings who had managed to fall foul of
the church. The weather was then so wild and wet, that the
Bishop tried to persuade his nephew to postpone his mission of
mercy. An obstinate determination was obviously one of the
keystones of Gerald's character, so he set out as he had planned,
making his famous observation that only the prospect of a sea
journey should compel a man to alter his plans on account of the
weather.

In quiet weather, Carew is the gentlest of all Welsh riverside
castles. Here there are no forbidding cliffs, only wide meadows
sloping gradually to the water. But as Gerald experienced, and as
Turner showed in a painting of 1832, the place can glower and

threaten under storm clouds. The story goes that Gerald's beautiful grandmother, Princess Nest, the Helen of Wales, still walks along the battlements that were her dowry. However, the castle that she knew no longer exists; and only one tower remains of the building that replaced it in 1192, and which was to become a fortified Tudor manor house, home of Sir John Perrot, reputedly an illegitimate son of Henry VIII. The smoke from the fires in his great hall was carried away by tall, round chimneys of a Flemish design, that are a peculiar feature of the vernacular architecture of this part of Pembrokeshire. Only a few survive, for many of them became quarries for other buildings, or were dismantled so that the stone could be ground down as a buffing powder for wooden plates and bowls.

Although both Nest and Gerald would find Carew's ruins strange, they would recognise the early eleventh-century cross that stands on the lane at the entrance to the castle grounds. It towers over thirteen feet, and is heavily decorated with swirling interlaced patterns, which the Celts may well have inherited from the Moorish North African travellers, who sailed the Atlantic seaboard. This cross is thought to commemorate a gift of castle land to the church; and that seems appropriate, for despite its elaborate decorations it somehow gives the impression of a pompous legal document.

Walk D: Carew to Cresswell (OS sheet 158)

In fine weather, this relatively little known area is so lovely that it is worthwhile walking to the ruins of another fortified manor on the banks of Carew's twin river, the Cresswell. The way goes north through fields to the west of Carew Castle, and so joins the lane to Cresswell Quay, which still bears signs of its industrial past. The way to the sixteenth-century ruins of Cresswell Castle goes through riverside bluebell woods, carpeted in spring with a gentle mist of anemones. Four towers still remain on the north bank of this river, the substantial remains of a fortified waterside dwelling.

Lamphey

From Carew, the lanes run south to the ruins of the Bishop's Palace of Lamphey. In the fourteenth century, the fish ponds, orchards and well-stocked gardens of this sheltered retreat, provided the Bishop of St David's with an earthly pastoral paradise in which almost anything would flourish and flower, as the astounding row of palm trees that grow on its outer wall now testify. Gerald, who knew Lamphey well, albeit at a time when its pleasures were not so fully developed, tells of the part it played in the Norman–Welsh skirmishes of 1096. At that time, his grandfather, Gerald de Windsor, severely oppressed by the Welsh who had besieged him in Pembroke Castle, put a brilliant plan into operation and so succeeded in deflecting his attackers. When his garrison had all but run out of food, he

> *caused four hogs, which yet remained, to be cut into*
> *small pieces and thrown down to the enemy from the*

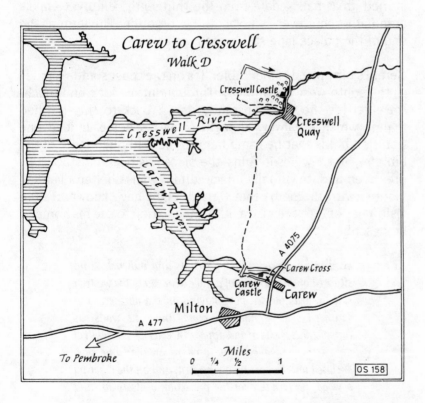

> *fortifications. The next day, having again recourse to a more refined stratagem, he contrived that a letter sealed with his own signet should be found before the house of Wilfred, bishop of St David's, who was then by chance in that neighbourhood, as if accidentally dropped, stating that there would be no necessity of soliciting the assistance of Earl Arnulph for the next four months to come. The contents of these letters being made known to the army, the troops abandoned the siege of the castle, and retired to their own homes.*

Bishop Wilfred's palace at Lamphey was a simple timber-frame building which has now completely disappeared. The earliest remains among the present ruins – the walls of a two-storied great hall – date from the thirteenth century. Gerald's grandfather, however, is not entirely forgotten. The farm at the end of the palace lane still bears his name.

Manorbier

Gerald's birthplace of Manorbier lies on the coast some six miles to the south-west of Lamphey. Throughout his long and much-travelled life, he was constantly drawn back to this fortified manor, which he always thought of as his home. Indeed one tradition holds that he came here to die. Although most of the building he knew lies in ruins, the place has been most lovingly preserved and its virtually intact curtain-walls shelter a garden, planted with the herbs that Gerald might have known. So the visitor has only to exercise a little imagination to see his home as he described it:

> *excellently well defended by turrets and bulwarks, and situated on the summit of a hill extending to the western side towards the sea-port, having on the northern and southern sides a fine fish pond under its walls, as conspicuous for its grand appearance, as for the depth of its waters, and a beautiful orchard on the same side, enclosed on one part by a vineyard, and on the other by a wood, remarkable for the projection of its rocks, and*

*the height of its hazel trees. On the right hand of the
promontory, between the castle and the church, near the
site of a very large lake and mill, a rivulet of never-
failing water flows through a valley rendered sandy by
the violence of the winds. Towards the west, the Severn
Sea, bending its course to Ireland, enters a hollow bay at
some distance from the castle; and the southern rocks, if
extended a little further towards the north, would render
it a most excellent harbour for shipping . . . This
country is well supplied with corn, sea-fish, and
imported wines; and what is preferable to every other
advantage, from its vicinity to Ireland, it is tempered by
a salubrious air . . . It is evident, therefore, that
Maenor Pirr is the pleasantest spot in Wales; and the
author may be pardoned for having thus extolled his
native soil, his genial territory, with a profusion of praise
and admiration.*

Lake and fish pond have gone, so have the orchards and
woods; and Manorbier's present curator is quick to point out that
Colt Hoare's Latinity must have let him down over the vineyards,
for she has heard of people who have come to grief in trying to
grow grapes on the sandy shores of this frequently storm-tossed
inlet. However, even if the wine were always imported, Manorbier
still exudes that air of gracious plenty which Gerald described.

The solar, in which he was born, lies above the twelfth-century
great hall, which was later to be embellished with a Flemish
round chimney, which is still in place. It was in that hall that
Gerald's favourite older brother, Philip, fell into confusion
because the laws of hospitality forced him to entertain the rich
travellers journeying between Milford and Devon. They made
such demands on his hospitality that he found he could no
longer afford to help the poor people at his gates. Wondering
where his Christian duty lay in such a predicament, he turned to
his clerical brother for guidance. Gerald gave the convenient,
statesmanlike answer. Both rich and poor were equally entitled
to Philip's bounty, a decree confirmed by the Pope, who granted

the Lord of Manorbier a dispensation for the cost of entertaining wealthy pilgrims.

In the chapel, to the east end of the great hall, there is an ancient niche, partly blocked by a medieval chimney-fitting. The curator believes that at one time a statue or bust of Gerald may have stood there. However that may be, a likeness of the great man, which may well have been made in his lifetime, can still be seen in this district. It is fixed to a cottage wall on the western edge of Angle Bay, where Gerald once held the living.

Pembrokeshire Coast Path (OS sheets 158 and 157)

Angle Bay is reached either by going directly west from Pembroke or by following the officially designated Pembroke-shire Coast Path. It goes round Manorbier beach, where Gerald remembered building sand cathedrals as a child, while his older brothers were busy with more conventional castles. The Coast Path follows the inlets round the amazing shapes that the waves have carved out of the sheer limestone cliffs for some twelve miles to Bosherston, where the walker must go inland if the army's red flag is flying.

When there is no firing, it is possible to go a little further west round the headland to the rock-girt chapel of St Govan, a simple, fifteenth-century mud-floored cell by a holy healing well. From here the Coast Path is forced inland by the artillery range, and follows the B 4319 to Castlemartin and Broomhill Burrows. From there the road to Angle goes past a bronze-age burial cyst, significant enough to be known as The Devil's Quoit, an indication of the long history of settlement here.

Angle (OS sheet 157)

There is a ruined peel tower in Angle village, and nearby is the stone head ascribed to Gerald and believed to have been brought here from St David's. At this treacherous entrance to Milford Haven, this little harbour also gives space to a charnel house, where drowned sailors lay awaiting burial. It is a macabre little building, which may excuse a reference to the ghost stories that Gerald had to tell of his homeland.

One of these specifically relates to the house of Orielton (955993), which lies off the road between Angle and Pembroke. It now belongs to the Field Studies Council, and has been totally rebuilt since Gerald knew it. A magnificently elegant eighteenth-century edifice raised over a Tudor basement has replaced the home of the Wiriet family, of whom Gerald had this eerie tale to tell:

Orielton (OS sheet 158)

> In the house of Stephen [Wiriet] the spirit in a most extraordinary manner conversed with men, and, in reply to their taunts, upbraided them openly with everything they had done from their birth, and which they were not willing should be known or heard by others.

Gerald's predeliction for tales of the supernatural was more than matched by his almost English delight in strange animal stories. So he would have enjoyed meeting Ronald Lockley, who lived at Orielton in the 1950s, and whose biological researches there led to the publication of *The Private Life of the Rabbit*, a source book for *Watership Down*.

One of the best of Gerald's own animal anecdotes comes from Pembroke Castle, where a man living in the bailey

Pembroke Castle

> found a brood of young weasels concealed within a fleece in his dwelling house, which he carefully removed and hid. The mother, irritated at the loss of her young, which she had searched for in vain, went to a vessel of milk that had been set aside for the use of the master's son, and raising herself up, polluted it with her deadly poison; thus revenging, as it were, the loss of her young by the destruction of the child. The man, observing what had passed, carried the fleece back to its former place; when the weasel, agitated by maternal solicitude, between hope and fear, on finding her young, began to testify her joy by cries and actions, and returning quickly to the

vessel, overthrew it; thus, in gratitude for the recovery of her own offspring, saving that of her host from danger.

From Angle and Orielton, the B 4320 enters Pembroke from the south-west, so the traveller will find that the castle, in which Henry Tudor, Duke of Richmond, was born in 1457, stands to the left of the cobbled street descending into the town. Almost four hundred years before Henry's birth, Arnulf de Montgomery, in an endeavour to subdue both the Welsh and the Vikings, fortified this rock above the river with a castle of staves and turves. It was still only 'a slender fortress' when Gerald knew it; and it was certainly no impregnable bastion that his grandfather, Gerald de Windsor, was left to defend after the Montgomery had returned to his own side of the border. De Windsor owed his frequently unenviable position as permanent castellian of Pembroke to various political manoeuvrings after his lovely wife, Nest, had borne a bastard son to Henry I.

In 1138, the earldom of Pembroke was created for Gilbert de Clare, known to history as Strongbow. It was he who enlarged the castle, which was then used as a base for his son Richard's excursions into Ireland. The ruined walls that tower now above the pathway beside the river were first put in place by that Richard's son-in-law, William Marshall. It was he who built the fine tower, still standing, in which the founder of the Tudor monarchy was born.

Newgale Sands (OS *sheet* 157)

All this is a digression, abetted by Gerald, from the main course of Baldwin's journey towards St David's, a route that followed the present B 4330 from Haverfordwest to Camrose and Newgale although, even when Colt Hoare was writing, the more direct route to the north-west, now the A 487, had become a major turnpike. Camrose church, crowned by a large white weathercock is dedicated to St Ishmael, which appropriately brings Caradoc back to mind, for Gerald writes of a miracle that occurred in 1124 when that holy man's corpse was carried over the long stretch of Newgale Sands to be buried at St David's. As the cortège wound along the shore 'a prodigious fall of rain inundated the whole country; but the conductors of the sacred burthen, on coming forth from their shelter, found the silken pall, with which the bier was covered, dry and uninjured by the storm'.

Fifty years later another violent storm hit Newgale and, as Gerald wrote, revealed a sunken forest when

> *the surface of the earth, which had been covered for many ages, reappeared, and discovered the trunks of trees cut off, standing in the very sea itself, the strokes of the hatchet appearing as if only made yesterday. The soil was very black, and the wood like ebony. By a wonderful revolution, the road for ships became impassable, and looked, not like a shore, but like a grove cut down, perhaps, at the time of the deluge, or not long after, but certainly in very remote ages, being by degrees consumed and swallowed up by the violence and encroachments of the sea.*

The accuracy of Gerald's account is borne out by the drowned forest that can be seen on the beach below Marros, some ten miles east of Tenby. There, just such trunks of long-submerged oak and silver birch have been partially preserved by accumulated layers of blue clay and peat, so that their embalmed roots are visible at low tide.

Storms still sweep Newgale beach, as they must have done when one of Caradoc's medieval followers settled as an anchorite by this shore in order to fulminate in prophecy against the enemies of St David's. Now the road is liable to flood, when the great protecting wall of pebbles swept up by successive tides gets scattered by the storm waves and the sea pounds inland to the water-meadows.

From Newgale, the road climbs steeply over the hill to descend *Solva* into the deep inlet of Solva, more like a Norwegian fjord than the estuary of a Welsh river. The Viking invaders must have felt that they were coming home when they moored their longboats here. Even now this unusual landscape makes it much easier to imagine the arrival of the Norsemen in Solva than to envisage the departure of those nineteenth-century Welsh men and women, who left this harbour for the promised land of America at the emigrant's fare of £3.10s a head. Holiday boats throng the harbour now, but Solva still bears the more vital marks of its industrial history in the quarries which tunnel under its eastern hill.

Pembrokeshire Coast Path

Another stretch of the Pembrokeshire Coast Path runs from the west of Solva to Porthstinian. It is an arduous walk of more than fifteen miles, but anyone who wants to shorten the way will find several lanes leading from the coast to St David's. But the whole walk is worth all the scrambling along the cliff-tops, the climbs up the steep sides of the inlets, and the strenuous adventures to reach wind-swept earthworks of coastal forts on rocky headlands. The coastal moors are covered with heather, low gorse bushes and bracken through which the narrow footpath winds almost imperceptibly. To the south, the wide expanse of St Brides Bay carries the eye round to the outpost of Skomer island.

St Non's

It is certainly worth making a short detour inland to visit St Non's chapel (754243). Non was the mother of David, and she is said to have given birth to the saint on this wild coast as a thunderstorm shook the sky. The vestigial ruins of the chapel that was built in her honour have not been dated, but there is no doubt that a succession of pilgrim shrines were raised at the place where the present stones stand, carefully fenced off from the grazing bullocks. In the south-east corner of this small enclosure there is an upright stone incised with a wheel-cross, which has been venerated for over a thousand years, although there is no direct evidence to prove that it has always stood on this site. Near the chapel the saint's holy well is carefully preserved in a little walled garden.

Pilgrims who came to the chapel and the well landed at the tiny inlet of Porth Clais just to the west. They came to pay their respects to St Non before setting out on the last stage of their journey to the shrine of her son. Nor were they the only seafarers to land on this stretch of coast. According to one story in the *Mabinogion*, Twrch Trwyth, the wild boar of Ireland, who killed the sons of Arthur, made his landfall here; and some hagiographers claim that it was from this miniscule port that St Patrick sailed to Ireland. More certainly it was an inlet for small trading vessels until comparatively recent times, as the remains of the coastal lime-kilns testify.

There is a short cut to be taken by anyone prepared to forego the view of Ramsey Island and the southern rocks from the cliffs of Pen Dal-aderyn. It cuts off the headland by running along the farm tracks to rejoin the Coast Path going north above Maen Bachau to the rocky harbour of Porthstinian, which also served as a landing place for pilgrims bound for St David's. This is no easy port. A string of rocks, justly called The Bitches, stretches out into the sound for Ramsey Island, and any boat hoping to land here has to run the gauntlet of their jagged teeth. Two years after Becket's murder, the contrite Henry II landed here on the Easter Monday, about noon according to Gerald's account, and from the landing place proceeded to the shrine of St David 'habited like a pilgrim and leaning on a staff'. Before he undertook that final stage of his penance, however, he may well have paused at the cliff-top chapel dedicated to St Justinian, the sixth-century hermit of Ramsey Island, in order to give thanks for a safe voyage. The present rectangular stone shell is of a later date, it is the ruin of a chapel built by the sixteenth-century Bishop Vaughan on the same site.

Porthstinian is not without its secular memories too. A few centuries back cattle were scrambling ashore here after being forced to swim for the mainland from their island pastures. Now the little port's most important function is to serve as a lifeboat station for a vessel whose crew is called out to its mission of rescue in some of the most treacherous waters around the British Isles. In fair weather it is also the place from which visitors can depart on seal and sea bird viewing cruises round the cliffs of Ramsey's western shore.

Porthstinian

In the twelfth century, the country inland from Porthstinian must have been a barren morass, and despite careful farming it is still rough and bleak. But the narrow lanes running through the farm enclosures have high banks covered in glowing toadflax and the rich red campion. This is Menevia, the cruel, but beautiful wasteland that David chose for his settlement. It is good to explore it further before joining Baldwin at Peter de Leia's cathedral.

Walk E: Porthstinian to Carn Llidi

From Porthstinian, the Coast Path goes round the mile-long shining beach of Whitesands Bay which covers another sunken forest. This bay formed the western end of a bronze-age trade route running from Stonehenge over the Preseli Hills and from here stone and metals were carried across the Irish sea. Sometime between the sixth and tenth centuries a chapel dedicated to St Patrick was set up here. It was excavated in 1821, and now lies beneath a mound of tangled grasses to the west of the footpath, as it leaves the beach for the headland.

Past the secluded sands of Porthmelgan, the path follows the contours round the heather-covered headland to the massive stone rampart which stretched across the neck of St David's Head to protect the iron-age farmers and warriors who lived at this western tip of the land. From here they looked across the swirling seas to the distant island of Grassholm, and from such a vantage point were able, in clear weather at least, to forestall sea-borne invasions; and it would be bold pirates indeed who ventured these rock-filled waters when the mists came down. Here are the evil islands known as the Bishop and his Clerks, which as the sixteenth-century Pembrokeshire writer, George Owen, observed, preached a 'deadly doctrine to their winter audiences'.

Another Arthur's Quoit, this time covering a burial chamber that could be fully five thousand years old, stands a few hundred yards to the north-east of the headland fort. Just beyond it a path climbs up to the rocks of Carn Llidi. From that height, from which it is possible to look west to the Wicklow Hills, the whole of the plain of Menevia spreads southwards to the single rock of Clegyr-

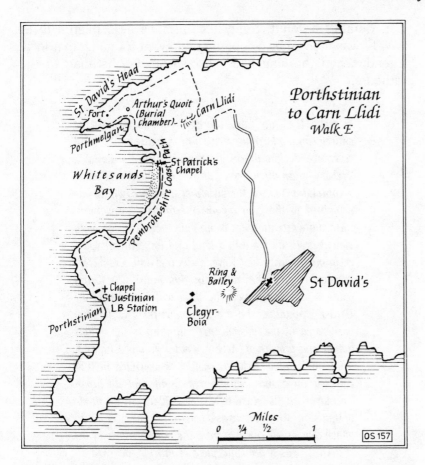

Boia (744252) the centre of a neolithic settlement on which a much later motte and bailey was set. Here legend is more fun than history. This hill may well have acquired its name from Boia, the heathen Celtic chieftain, but it is surely unlikely as the tale suggests that he was so desperate about the peaceable inroads of the Celtic missionaries that he got his wife to send her maids gambolling naked on the hillside in a fruitless endeavour to lure St David and his chaste monks into sin. According to that legend, divine retribution was swift. Boia's lady went mad, and he, himself, was destroyed with his entire household.

In Gerald's account, Henry II's entrance as a pilgrim to St David's was marked by a supernatural event to match that local legend. When the king had walked from Porthstinian to the cathedral

he met at the white gate a procession of the canons of the church coming forth to receive him with due honour and reverence. As the procession moved solemnly along, a Welsh woman threw herself at the king's feet, and made a complaint against the bishop of the place, which was explained to the king by an interpreter. The woman, immediate attention not being paid to her petition, with violent gesticulation and a loud and impertinent voice, exclaimed repeatedly. "Revenge us this day, Lechlaver! revenge us and the nation in this man!' On being chidden and driven away by those who understood the British language, she more vehemently and forcibly vociferated in the like manner, alluding to the vulgar fiction and proverb of Merlin, 'That a king of England, and conqueror of Ireland, should be wounded in that country by a man with a red hand and die upon Lechlaver, on his return to Menevia'. This was the name of that stone which serves as a bridge over the river Alun, which divides the cemetry from the northern side of the church. It was a beautiful piece of marble, polished by the feet of passengers, ten feet in length, six in breadth, and one in thickness. Lechlaver signifies in the British language a talking stone.

That stone got its name from the day when it burst into speech as a coffin was being carried across it. After that funeral processions chose to take a different route, but the king was made of sterner stuff and determined to make it abundantly clear that he was above such superstition. So, in a gesture of defiance at the mythology that inspired much of the Welsh resistance to the English monarch, he paused only a moment before stepping on to the portentious marble and declaring that after his action nobody need take notice of Merlin's prophecies.

The modern pilgrim, who decides to follow Henry and enter the cathedral from the open country to the west, must also cross the Alun river, which flows between it and the magnificent towering arches of the Bishop's Palace. There is a choice of two pretty little bridges across the water here, but no sign of the marble slab. The Lechlaver has vanished, and Henry II would seem to have made his point.

The cathedral which Baldwin came to was still incomplete. The sadly unpopular Peter de Leia was putting all his energies into constructing a large cruciform building on the site of the Celtic monastic buildings which Gerald's uncle had presided over. De Leia's work on his new cathedral was not to be completed for another ten years, but by 1188 much of his vision had been realised. Apart from the decorated arches in the nave, it is however, no longer present to the eyes of the modern pilgrim. De Leia's low central tower collapsed in 1220, and in 1248 an earthquake almost completed the damage. So most of the present building dates from the fourteenth century. Yet there are vestiges of the much earlier church in this hidden hollow. Here is a stone commemorating Bishop Abraham, who was killed by Viking marauders in 1081 together with his two sons, Hedd and Isaac, a reminder of the Celtic church's tolerance of married clergy, which sent Gerald into such a frenzy of distaste. He would be better pleased by the modern notice on the outside of the south door forbidding visitors to bring their dogs into this sacred place.

Amusingly enough, the effigy of Gerald, put up at the behest of Victorian worthies, whose clergy were notoriously uxorious and philoprogenitive, has an expression of tight-lipped disapproval. There he stands, opposite the relics of Justinian and David, sternly chagrined that the mitre he never achieved lies for ever at his feet. In 1188, he unbent a little, at least sufficiently to be grateful for the hospitality that Peter de Leia provided, and to describe his rival as a 'liberal man'.

The palace where Baldwin was entertained has been reduced

to the western range of the present lordly ruin. The vaulting in the undercroft of that twelfth-century remnant gives some idea, however, of the splendour that the Archbishop enjoyed. Yet it must surely have been an uneasy visit, only a little while previously the canons of St David's had tried their best to persuade Lord Rhys to prevent Baldwin from setting foot in their diocese.

For totally non-political reasons, the modern visitor may share some of this unease. Cathedral and palace, set in rural magnificence by fields where the glossy Welsh black cattle graze, have all the enchantment and significance of a long-hallowed place. A climb up the steps from the south door to the archway that leads to the little city dispels it all. Here is a place submerged beneath the weight of tourism and its demands. Real life must go on here – there is at least a school to prove it – but it is hard to detect. Better to take the road again and follow Baldwin to Lord Rhys's castle in Cardigan.

CHAPTER SIX

St David's to Strata Florida

Gerald did not accompany Baldwin on the road from St David's to Cardigan. He was left behind to preach to the people of Cemais, the rugged land flanked by the fearsome cliffs of Cardigan Bay to the north and the lovely ridge of the Preselis to the south. So he was able to make a more leisurely way to his meeting with the Archbishop at St Dogmaels Abbey on the banks of the Teifi.

Cemais

There are three ways to follow him there. The first, and in many ways the most obviously enjoyable, is to follow the long bewitching spell of the north Pembrokeshire Coast Path. The second is to head south, and delight in the splendour of the Preseli ridgeway, running across hills whose modest height is disguised by the drama of the rocks that crown them. The third route is both the most authentic and the most prosaic. It leaves St David's by the busy, lead-fumes-and-petrol-flavoured A 487, whose tarmac covers the ancient Meidr-y-Sant (the lane of the saints), the original pilgrim overland route to St David's.

Fortunately it is possible to make the best of all three ways on the journey to the east. A couple of miles out of St David's, the A 487 is crossed at 769262 by a footpath which goes along the course of the Monk's Dyke. This trackway links the north and south coasts of the peninsula, and its way is now clearly marked by yellow guide posts. That is most helpful for as it goes north it runs through the marshy ground to the west of Dowrog Common, a reserve tended by the West Wales Naturalist Trust. This part of the old route joins a lane at Rhodiad-y-Brenin (the King's Walk), so called because of a tradition that William the Conqueror

Walk A: Monk's Dyke to Mathry (OS sheet 157)

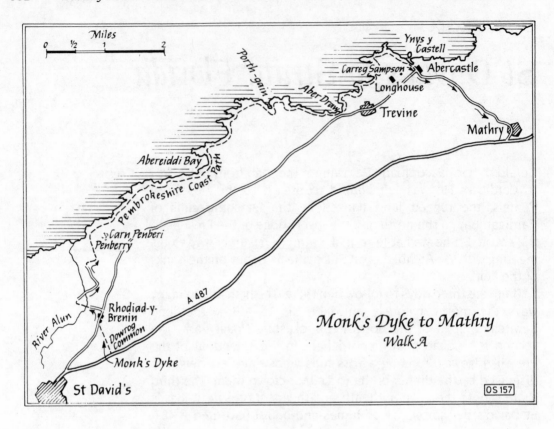

Monk's Dyke to Mathry
Walk A

OS 157

forestalled and upstaged Henry II by walking barefoot from here, when he went on pilgrimage to St David's.

A footpath leads off the lane to the north-east of the village, and crosses the diminutive River Alun by a stone clapper bridge to join a network of lanes of all ages, which zig-zag round the ancient route towards the rocky outcrop of Carn Penberi (Kite's Head Rock), a volcanic outcrop, similar in formation to that of Carn Llidi by St David's Head.

Carreg Sampson   This is a good place to join the Pembrokeshire Coast Path as it runs east above the cliff-tops to Abereiddi Bay, Porth-gain and

Aber Draw. On the western side of the inlet of Abercastle, a farm track goes inland to the precariously tilted, massive capstone of Carreg Sampson, which once supported a mound large enough to be a landmark for bronze-age sailors as well as providing an impressive tomb-covering for the illustrious dead.

Back on the path, the way goes to the narrow, sandy beach of *Abercastle* Abercastle, along the banks of a sea inlet, which provided a channel deep enough for nineteenth-century trading vessels from Bristol and Liverpool to moor and unload. The Coast Path reaches the little harbour after passing the remains of the lime-kilns, to which the ships once brought their freight of stone. The eastern side of the inlet is however the more dramatic and astonishing. Here the path slants up to the headland, where the walker is confronted by a sheer wall of black rock, rising out of the sea where Ynys y Castell broke away from the mainland. A little to the west is a vividly blue lagoon, the legacy of an abandoned coastal quarry. Yachts can be snugly moored there, but the racing currents round the broken-off island suggest that this is a berth for experienced sailors only.

A lane from Abercastle goes inland to Mathry, a pocket of *Mathry* fertile farmland, from which Gerald, who was once a prebendary here, drew rich tithes, in contrast to the meagre pickings that he got from Angle. Now Mathry is a small, but still prosperous, hill-top village, where large houses mingle with a row of pretty cottages whose roofs are weather-proofed by the sort of stone wash that is one of Pembrokeshire's many distinctive architectural signatures. Its immense church is not quite so pleasing. It has a large, presumptious apse built as late as 1867. However it stands on ground that has been sacred for centuries, as the inscribed burial stone in the church porch testifies.

The fertility of Mathry's farmlands has been enhanced, no doubt, by generous liming from the eighteenth century onwards; but this soil provided lush pasture and productive arable land long before the agricultural improvers got busy. The tithes that the Mathry farmers sent to St David's earned it the name of the 'golden prebend'. Yet, when Edward II granted the charter for the Mathry Michaelmas fair in 1356, the deed was witnessed by three English clerics led by the Archbishop of York, a blatant example of the neglect of the Welsh clergy, which had caused Gerald such distress two hundred years before.

Newport (OS *sheet* 145)

From Mathry, the obvious route to the east follows the main road to Fishguard, although it is, of course, quite possible to rejoin the Pembrokeshire Coast Path and make a tour round the massive Strumble Head. East from Fishguard, the Coast Path and trunk road A 487 meet at the holiday village of Newport, dominated in the sixteenth century by the geologist and local historian, George Owen, the eccentric squire from nearby Henllys. In fact this part of Cemais seems to have attracted autocratic rulers, for Newport's castle was originally built by the Norman Marcher lord, Martin of Tours, who was rewarded for his services to William at the conquest by a grant of rich coastal plain. He ruled the district with an absolute power, which was as effective in restraining the Welsh as it would have been had his domain covered the Marches of the English border. His descendants still hold the office of the Lords Marcher of Cemais, and have the right of appointing Newport's mayor, who in turn presides over the August meeting of the Court Leet which perambulates the bounds of the borough, an exercise which takes the civic party on a climb up to Preseli. History has not been so kind to the castle. In 1859, a spacious private house was built over its ruins, and now only the traces of a thirteenth-century gatehouse remain.

However, Newport is not short of folklore and history. This is the home of the game of Cnappen, vividly described by George Owen, who claimed that the Welsh had inherited it from the Trojans, when the legendary Brutus invaded Britain. However mythical its origin, the game was played with a very real, hard wooden ball and according to a flexible set of rules which allowed for contesting teams that could run into hundreds of players, some of whom were mounted – a practical necessity, as the goals could be up to eight miles apart. In later years it became a regular Shrove Tuesday ritual for the men of Newport to play the men of Nevern on the relatively restricted area of the beach.

It is very likely that Baldwin spent a night at Nevern Castle on his long journey from St David's to the banks of the Teifi. The castle stood on a hill above the church by the river, some four miles to the north-east of Newport; but anyone who wants to walk, for at least a little way on the Preselis, will not take that direct route. It is much more enticing to set off along the path which the Newport August procession takes as it beats the bounds as far as the rocks of Mynydd Carningli. An iron-age hill fort, it has a direct link with Nevern, whose founding saint, the sixth-century Brynach, had a vision of angels at this high place.

Walk B: Newport to Nevern by Pentre Ifan

From here it is impossible to resist walking across the valley to the east in order to reach the cromlech of Pentre Ifan, whose surviving stones have become a veritable logo for Preseli. Their impact never stales. This capstone was raised seven feet above a hundred-foot-long barrow sited in the most prominent position on the hillside. Who knows what rituals were practised here as men gazed out over an ocean of trees to the wide sea?

There is no need to return to Newport. A path goes downhill through the woods to the farm of Pentre Ifan, whose cattle graze disconsolately on the misty heights, and from there a lane runs to Llystyn, when a path goes west and then north to the A 487. Once across that obstacle, it is possible to walk in gentle country above the meander of the River Nyfer and so come to the woods that surround Nevern Castle.

Just before the path reaches the road, its way is barred by a stile set up beside a boulder that is marked with clearly defined foot-shaped steps, once used by pilgrims on their way diagonally across Wales from Holywell in the north-east to St David's. Beyond that boulder is an even more poignant reminder of the pilgrim route, a wall of bare rock in the hillside, embossed with a simple cross. The symbol seems to be actually growing out of the stone, and it is no wonder that tradition affirms that it was not made by human hands but appeared miraculously, together with

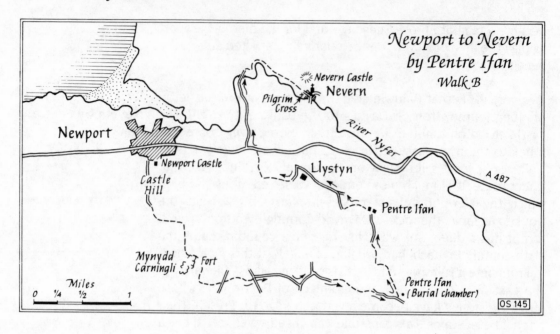

the little ledge beneath it, which provided a kneeling place for the devout to make their prayers.

Nevern Castle

The footpath meets the road at the bend of the hill. Above it are the remains of Nevern Castle, (Castell Nannyfer) earthworks of a classic motte and bailey, incorporating the natural cliffs of the hill into its defences, as its third-century predecessor had done. It is a beautifully tended place, the careful interpretation is never over-intrusive; and the bailey is filled with marshy reeds, while primrose flower along the banks where the pallisades once provided a final defence.

In 1191, Lord Rhys, whose daughter Angharad had made a diplomatic marriage with William, the Norman Lord of Cemais and grandson of Martin of Tours, attacked his son-in-law's stronghold here. Gerald could not resist adding that story to his notes when he came to write up his journey of 1188. Anticipating events by three years, he wrote that Rhys was incited to make the attack by his cunning son, Gruffydd, who subsequently lost the castle to 'the man in the world he most hated, his brother Malgon'.

Sickened by the treachery of his warring offspring, Lord Rhys then planned to disinherit Angharad and his grandchildren by her; but before he could put that intention into force, he was attacked by his sons Malgon and Hywel. They defeated their father, and for nearly a year held him an ignominious prisoner in Nevern Castle, a fate which Gerald attributed to divine justice. He found it fitting that his noble cousin should suffer 'the greatest disgrace and confusion in the very place where he had perpetrated an act of the most consummate baseness'. The ruined stone walls of Lord Rhys's prison are still standing round the rock of the inner castle, due west of the motte.

In 1188, that wretchedness all lay in the future. When Baldwin was entertained overnight in William of Tours' castle at Nevern, Lord Rhys, at the height of his powers, was preparing to receive the Archbishop and his entourage in his fine new castle at Cardigan. On the next stage of his journey to that stronghold, Baldwin had to ride downhill from Nevern to the site of the church by the river. It is reasonable to assume that he would have stopped there in order to preach by the thirteen-foot-high, tenth-century cross that stands among the magnificent yews of the churchyard, and whose lively interlacing patterns rival those of the Celtic cross at Carew.

Although most of Nevern church dates from the fifteenth century, its tower is much earlier and it contains two stones of even greater antiquity. These now form an interior windowsill to the south chapel. One is inscribed to the memory of the fifth-century Maglocunnus, son of Clotorus. His name is given in both Roman script and fifth-century Celtic Ogham, whose linear strokes are slashed across, above and beneath the angle formed by the edge of the stone and its flat surface. The rest of the sill is made up of a long, narrow slab on which a cross in low relief is formed out of carved cords forming a central knot.

Possibly these stones were known to the Irish Brynach, who founded the Christian settlement here in the sixth century. In the tradition of the Celtic church he was a married man, having taken for his wife one of the many saintly daughters of Brychan, king of Brecon. That was probably as convenient a territorial arrangement in its time as the secular, dynastic marriages that Lord Rhys made for his children. Indeed there is every reason to believe that it was a much happier and more harmonious arrangement than anything the Welsh prince contrived, but Gerald with his intense distaste for married clergy would be unlikely to agree.

From Nevern, the way to St Dogmaels and the River Teifi lies to the north-east, but Baldwin appears to have taken a more roundabout route, following the course of the River Nyfer south to Felindre Farchog, where it is joined by the stream of Nant Duad. At that place (104392), the nineteenth-century Richard Fenton, author of a *Historical Tour through Pembrokeshire*, noted the bridge of Pont y Baldwin.

The lanes to St Dogmaels

It is possible to take a pleasantly wooded waterside walk to Pont y Baldwin from Nevern, but at Felindre Farchog the path joins the A 487. So it is better to take the more northern course to the east, and follow the lanes, whose banks are so covered with toadflax that Gerald's odd, sad anecdote of Sisillus Longleg is soon brought to mind. This unfortunate, a contemporary of Gerald's

> suffered as violent a persecution from toads, as if the reptiles of the whole province had come to him by agreement; and though destroyed by his nurses and friends, they increased again on all sides in infinite numbers, like hydras' heads. His attendants, both friends and strangers, being wearied out, he was drawn up in a kind of bag into a high tree, stripped of its leaves and shred; nor was he there secure from his venemous enemies, for they crept up the tree in great numbers and consumed him even to the very bones.

Colt Hoare recorded that a house called Tre-liffan (Toad's Town) was to be found in Cemais, in which a marble sculpture of that creature graced the chimney-piece. Although the carving had been brought from Italy, Gerald's translator liked to think that it was set up to commemorate the fate of the wretched Sisillus. Perhaps he had the neat and well-ordered farmstead of Trellyfiant in mind. It lies at 085423, along the lanes that run between Nevern and Molygrove and so on to St Dogmaels.

At that Benedictine abbey, founded by Martin of Tours' son Robert in 1115, Gerald rejoined Baldwin, and they were both most comfortably lodged overnight. The present parish church of St Dogmaels has been built into the ruins of that abbey on the west bank of the Teifi. It contains another inscribed Ogham stone, said to commemorate a prince of North Wales who had been granted land in Pembrokeshire. That historic stone was discovered in 1858 embedded in the wall of the vicarage after it had served its turn as a footbridge across the stream that feeds the millpond. The story goes that a lady dressed in white still hovers by it, trying to walk over the water it once bridged. From such a wraith it is a pleasure to turn to the pleasingly corporeal ducks, waddling their way through the more secular parts of the river, or swimming in the pond that once more serves a working flour mill.

Cardigan

Across the Teifi from St Dogmaels, the modern town of Cardigan has grown up around the castle, which Lord Rhys built in 1171, on the site of a Norman fortification, whose custodian, Stephen, another lover of the beautiful Nest, lost to Lord Rhys's father in 1136. Forty years after that event, Lord Rhys himself organised the first Welsh eisteddfod, a series of competitions among bards and musicians of the sort that Henry II's Queen Eleanor was familiar with in her duchy of Aquitaine. He held it in the hall and grounds of his splendid new castle, which dominated the estuary of the Teifi as proudly as his Dynevor mastered Golden Grove.

Baldwin and Gerald both preached in Cardigan, and to such effect that

> *many were induced to take the cross; one of whom was*
> *an only son and the sole comfort of his mother, far*

advanced in years, who, steadfastly gazing on him, as if inspired by the Deity, uttered these words: 'O, most beloved Lord Jesus Christ, I return thee hearty thanks for having conferred on me the blessing of bringing forth a son, whom thou mayest think worthy of thy service.' Another woman at Aberteivi, of a very different way of thinking, held her husband fast by his cloak and girdle, and publicly and audaciously prevented him from going to the archbishop to take the cross; but three nights afterwards, she heard a terrible voice saying, 'Thou hast taken away my servant from me, therefore what thou most lovest shall be taken away from thee.' On her relating this vision to her husband, they were struck with mutual terror and amazement; and on falling asleep again, she unhappily overlaid her little boy, whom, with more affection than prudence, she had taken to bed with her. The husband, relating to the bishop of the diocese both the vision and its fatal prediction, took the cross, which his wife spontaneously sewed on her husband's arm.

Near the bridge where that sermon was delivered, the site of a memorial chapel was marked out. Gerald tells us that it was a well-known fact that many miracles were performed at the spot when Baldwin spoke, but, alas, he found it too tedious to relate the wondrous cures that took place there.

There is now no sign of the chapel that was built in the place where Baldwin preached his stirring recruiting sermon to the people of Cardigan, in the presence of Lord Rhys and his treacherous, quarrelsome sons, Malgon and Gruffydd. However Colt Hoare knew of a place called Chapelfield on the western bank of the Teifi and identified it with the commemorative site. He knew a small building set in a circular Celtic churchyard, somewhat upstream from the present bridge, and sadly demolished by the builders of the railway in 1859.

The area has not completely shaken off its Crusader associations for all the destruction of the Baldwin chapel. Admittedly there is no longer any trace of the hospice run by the Knights Templars that once stood in this area; but the asylum managed by their rival brother order, the Hospitallers of St John, is recalled by the naming of the Angel Hotel, which stands on its site, hidden in a maze of side-streets between the river and the ring road, and overshadowed by a locked, forbidding church.

It is a pity that Gerald lacked the magnanimity to leave some record of the miracles which he said were performed at the place where the modest Baldwin preached. Perhaps he was jealous, and not only on his own account, that such wonders should come out of Canterbury. Why ever it was, he found space and time to turn his attention instead to the fascination of the Teifi, and to devote the best part of a chapter to the salmon and beaver which abounded there in his day.

The beaver have sadly long gone, but the salmon remain, and so do the coracles which Gerald knew so well, and whose construction he outlined in his *Description of Wales*, explaining that these boats

> *are made of twigs, not oblong nor pointed, but almost round, or rather triangular, covered both within and without with raw hides. When a salmon thrown into one of these boats strikes it hard with his tail, he often oversets it, and endangers both the vessel and its navigator.*

Perhaps, it is for that reason that these frail light craft are not often used for salmon fishing. Indeed they are now almost entirely pleasure boats; serious fishing goes on along the inter-tidal reaches of the Teifi estuary, whose sands are marked by the poles which hold the nets in which the fish are trapped.

Gerald's digression on the beaver is excuse enough to follow the bends of the river inland to Cilgerran and Cenarth. A pleasantly gentle woodland path goes south from Cardigan's Wildlife Park, where visitors can see examples of the birds and animals that inhabit the area now. The path comes out by the church into

Walk C: Cardigan to Cilgerran (a circular walk), (OS sheet 145)

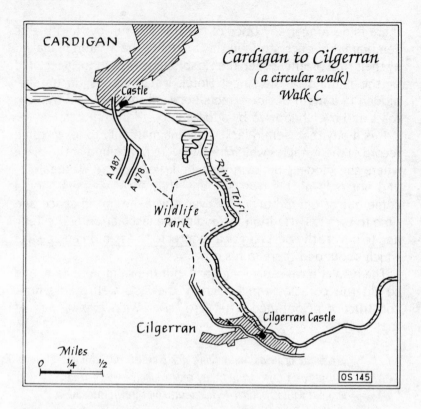

Cilgerran, a large village whose main street leads to a rocky gorge surmounted by the ruins of the castle captured by Lord Rhys in 1164. The outer ward of that twelfth-century bailey can be best appreciated from the dramatic river path that winds beneath the cliffs north towards Cardigan.

Every August, the river community stages a coracle festival and regatta at Cilgerran and its neighbouring village of Cenarth. These craft, whose construction Gerald described, still show an extraordinary manoeuvrability and versatility in the rapid turbulence of these waters. The modern coracles retain the ancient form, but their sides are covered with pitch-impregnated calico supplied by the drapers of Cardigan. But alas, it seems that their days are finally numbered, as the cost of coracle licenses rises prohibitively.

Cenarth, a little further up-river, is almost too well beloved by
tourists who flock to its magnificent bridge and to the tumbled
rocks over which the water flows swiftly from the east in shallow
but rapid cataracts. Gerald, who praised the quality of the
salmon here, cribbed from his own *Topography of Ireland* to explain
to his readers the way the fish negotiate such obstacles. To the
east of the bridge the waters are quieter, and it may have been
from here that Gerald was able to observe how the beavers

Cenarth

> *use such skill in the construction of their habitations
> that not a drop of water can penetrate, or the force of
> storms shake them; nor do they fear any violence but
> that of mankind, nor even that, unless well armed. They
> entwine the branches of willows with other wood, and
> different kinds of leaves, to the usual height of the water,
> and having made within-side a communication from
> floor to floor, they elevate a kind of stage, or scaffold,
> from which they may observe and watch the rising of the
> waters. In the course of time, their habitations bear the
> appearance of a grove of willow trees, rude and natural
> without, but artfully constructed within.*

Although the beaver are now extinct and the evidence of their
willow dams has long disappeared from the banks of the river,
Cenarth, despite its crowds of visitors, is still as enchanting as
Gerald found it when he listed its 'church dedicated to St Ludoc,
the mill, bridge, salmon leap, an orchard with a delightful garden'
all standing 'together on a small plot of ground'. Nothing is
known for certain of St Ludoc, to whom the church at Cilgerran is
also dedicated, but a tradition persists that he actually formed a
salmon trap in the rocks by hollowing out one of the stones with
his bare hand.

The southern meanders of the Teifi were not however on
Baldwin's itinerary. His way lay to the north-east. So when his
cavalcade left Lord Rhys's castle at Cardigan, it set out for Pont
Stephen or Lampeter, leaving 'Crugmore i.e. the great hill near

Crugmore

Aberteivi' on their left (2044751). Although this is not the highest hill in a fairly undulating terrain (it only rises a little over 400 feet) it is distinctive enough to stand out from miles away. It lies in private land, so it is not possible to climb up to the triangulation pillar that crowns it or more interestingly to look for the tumulus, which Gerald claimed gave rise to a local belief that it would 'adapt itself to persons of all stature; and that if any armour is left there entire in the evening, it will be found, according to vulgar tradition, broken to pieces in the morning'.

Colt Hoare confirms the existence of that tumulus, surrounded by some sort of entrenchment.

Baldwin probably passed through the village of Betws Ifan (302475), whose name links it to the Hospitallers of St John and the memory of the crusades. This means that he would have taken a route somewhat to the north of the present B 4333, and from there turned south-east towards Lampeter, where he and Gerald were joined by two Cistercian abbots, John of Whitland, whose abbey they had already visited, and Seisyll of Strata Florida, whither they were bound. All four clerics preached by this bridge across the Teifi and 'many persons were induced to take the cross'. From there they made their way north towards the river's source in swampy ground near Strata Florida.

Llanddewi-Brefi

On their way to Strata Florida, they must have passed through Llanddewi-Brefi, but Gerald writes as though the Archbishop's party came to that hill-top church after spending some days in the abbey to the north. It is difficult to see why Baldwin should have doubled back on his tracks in this way. Neither Colt Hoare nor Lewis Thorpe (Gerald's most recent translator) query the route given in the original, but I suspect that somehow the author of the *Itinerary* had managed to get his notes in a muddle here.

In any case, anyone following Baldwin's route now is bound to reach Strata Florida by way of Llanddewi-Brefi; and Gerald was certainly more concerned with the events that brought St David here in 519, than with Baldwin's subsequent visit. He explained that this church of St David is

> *situated on the summit of that hill which had formerly risen up under his feet whilst preaching, during the period of that celebrated synod, when all the bishops, abbots and clergy of Wales, and many other persons, were collected there on account of the Pelagian heresy, which although formerly exploded from Britain by Germanus, bishop of Auxerre, had lately been revived in these parts. At this place David was reluctantly raised to the archbishopric, by the unanimous consent and election of the whole assembly, who by loud acclamations testified their admiration of so great a miracle.*

The story of that miracle has been put into verse of our own time by Moelwyn Merchant, priest, sculptor and poet, who dismisses the Pelagian heresy of salvation by will power in lines which declare 'That bootstraps are not for lifting,/ That grace is humbler gear.'

The miracle which so impressed Gerald is paralleled (if that is the word to describe spontaneous risings of the ground) by a later elevation of the earth which took place in Scotland to the east of Dumfries. When Kentigern (Glasgow's St Mungo) came there on his return from Wales in 573, the crowd of people anxious to hear him speak was so vast, that the majority of his audience would have been unable to catch a glimpse of him had not the ground he was standing on suddenly and obligingly elevated itself. Then the whole multitude could see the saint, who is said to have been responsible for the founding of St Asaph cathedral, whither Baldwin was ultimately bound.

Llanddewi-Brefi is a sizeable village now, almost a small town. The thirteenth-century church stands on its slight hill above a neat square. From here the road runs north towards Strata Florida, skirting the 2,000-acre Tregaron Bog, managed by the Nature Conservancy as a breeding ground for numerous rare species of marsh plants and wildfowl. This extensive raised wetland was created when glacial debris filled a lake through which the Teifi flowed, a geological disturbance that might have caused the formation of the hill on which the church of Llanddewi-Brefi stands, for as Merchant wrote in his poem about David's miracle, 'Geology is never simple, nor for that matter very convenient'.

Strata Florida (OS
sheet 147)

When Baldwin and Gerald came to Strata Florida the abbey was still on its old site, a mile or so to the south-west of the present ruins. When a group of Cistercian monks from Whitland came to this northern wilderness in 1164, 'through the will of God and the instigation of the Holy Spirit' as the annals of the *Red Book of Hengest* recorded, they settled by Nant Lluest, a tributary of the Teifi, in the meadows of what is now Old Abbey Farm, and so gave its name to the present village of Pontrhydfendigaid (732665) – the bridge of the blessed ford. It was not until the eve of Pentecost in 1201 that they were to enter their new and splendid church, whose arch still frames the hills of the green desert of Wales where their sheep grazed. Among these ruins are the graves of many of the princes of Wales, including Lord Rhys's son, Malgon.

The abbey in which Baldwin stayed was founded on land granted by Gerald's uncle, Robert Fitz Stephen, the son of Nest and the constable of Cardigan. When Lord Rhys took that castle in 1166, he undertook responsibility for the monastery, of which his defeated enemy had been the patron, and procured such great resources for the foundation that the new building was able to take place on a magnificent scale. By 1184, Lord Rhys was in a position to grant a charter to the monks, confirmed by Henry II, which presented them with all the land from the slopes of Plinlimmon to the banks of the Wye at Rhayader.

True to their tradition the Strata Florida Cistercians had chosen one of the wildest and most desolate parts of Wales in which to settle. By their labour and ingenuity they were to transform it into rich pasture for herds of goats and flocks of sheep. Yet their industry was not wholly beneficent, as Leland noted when he came to describe the country around the abbey in the sixteenth century. He found, to his dismay, that although 'Many hilles thereabout hath bene well woddid, as evidently by old rotes apperith, but now in them is almost no wode – the causes be these: first the wood cut down was never copised, and this hath beene a great cause of destruction of wood through Wales. Secondly, after cutting down of woodys, the gottys hath so bytten the young spring that it never grew but lyke shrubbes. Thirdely, men for the monys destroied the great woddis that their should not harborow thieves.'

If, indeed, Baldwin was advised to retrace his steps so as to return to the south and approach Llanbadarn Fawr by way of that section of the Sarn Helen which runs well to the west of the Tregaron Bog and goes due north from the Teifi on the route now covered by the B 4578 (OS sheet 146), it may well have been for fear of brigands and Welsh extremists who might be lying in ambush in the still wooded hills in order to attack the English archbishop.

However it seems much more likely that such caution was extreme, and that Baldwin made his crossing of the Teifi by the bridge at Pontrhydfendigaid and so went north-west to cross the Ystwyth and the Rheidol. On that track he would be following the ancient route from Rhayader to the coast, a highway which played a significant part in the siting of Strata Florida. Although we cannot be certain which way he went, Gerald tells us that he had not gone far on his journey when he met Rhys's son, Cyneuric.

> This young man was of fair complexion, with curled hair, tall and handsome; clothed only according to the custom of his country, with a thin cloak and inner garment, his legs and feet, regardless of thorns and thistles, were left bare; a man, not adorned by art, but nature; bearing in his presence an innate, not an acquired, dignity of manners. A sermon having been preached to these three young men, Gruffydd, Malgon and Cyneuric, in the presence of their father, prince Rhys, and the brothers disputing about taking the

> *cross, at length Malgon strictly promised that he would*
> *accompany the Archbishop to the king's court, and*
> *would obey the king's and the Archbishop's counsel,*
> *unless prevented by them.*

In fact none of Lord Rhys's sons ventured to the Holy Land. Malgon somehow managed to squirm out of his commitment; Gruffydd was far too busy feathering his own nest; while the beautiful Cyneuric, according to the historian Sir John Lloyd, let nothing disturb 'his long life of dignified inaction'.

The monastery of Strata Florida was to play an important part in Gerald's life for years to come. In 1199, after the death of Peter de Leia, he chose to set out from here on the start of his journey to Rome where he was bound to seek the Pope's support for his campaign to become at least Bishop of St David's and possibly Archbishop of the church in Wales. Before leaving on his travels in that year, he deposited his books for safe keeping with the monks of Strata Florida, a move that was to cause much bitterness, as the lending of books so often will. In his *Speculum Ecclesiae*, which he wrote in 1220, he told what happened when he went to collect his library on his return from Rome, and of the indignation that he felt when the monks informed him that their *Book of Uses* only allowed them to buy books, not to hold them in pawn. So he was forced to leave his books 'to their greed as if his entrails had been torn from his belly, seeing such priceless treasures gathered for so long with such loving care commuted to cheap cash'.

Walk D: Strata Florida to Abbey Cwmhir (OS sheet 147)

The track that Gerald followed on his way to Abbey Cwmhir and the English border, eleven years after his visit to Strata Florida with Baldwin, is the eastern part of the ancient track from Mid Wales to the sea. It can still be followed, but this is not a walk to be attempted without a compass, for even in clear weather it is easy to get lost among the confusing waves of these barren hills. It is easy to understand that one of the worst restrictions which Gerald had to endure, after his activities had led him to fall foul of powerful church authorities, was to be deprived of a guide in his native Wales. This territory demands the sort of respect from the traveller that a true desert or an ocean calls for. The way is not made any easier by the marshy ground of the valleys and streams feeding the great reservoirs that are the source of Birmingham's water supply, and which can often force the walker to make wide detours from the planned route.

The way to the east starts along the lane to the north of the abbey, and then winds up to the Teifi lakes, marshy pools in the hills, where the river has its source. Thence it goes due east to cross the Claerwen, from which it rises to a clear ridgeway towards the Elan, which must be crossed by the new road bridge, constructed when the valley was flooded. Here the old way east joins the mountain road linking Rhayader and Aberystwyth, plunging back into the heather, as the road turns south. The ancient track heads from here to the sheer dramatic cliffs of Llofftyddgleision and the drop to the Wye valley. These rocks are so precipitous, that although the ancient way runs along the top of them, in a mist it is wiser to take the lower path.

The way to Rhayader lies south, through wooded lanes to the western bank of the Wye. From there, those who would follow Gerald further on that journey must take the lane going north-east into the hills towards Yr Onnen farm (034685) and so climb round the hill to reach the forest paths which lead to the clearing where a few stones stand to remind the visitor of the great Cistercian Abbey of Cwmhir, where the headless body of Llewel-lyn, one of the last great princes of independent Wales, killed at Builth in 1282, lies buried before the site of the high altar.

Baldwin's travels took him in another direction. He had to continue his journey northwards from Strata Florida by making for the religious settlement of Llanbadarn Fawr, a mile or so inland from the Ystwyth estuary and now a suburb of Aberyst-wyth. Its formidable much restored church, solid and almost totally unadorned, contains a number of intricately designed Celtic crosses, which Gerald must have seen when he came to the earlier church built on the site of St Padarn's sixth-century monastery. In 1188, the community at Llanbadarn Fawr still

Llanbadarn Fawr (OS *sheet* 135)

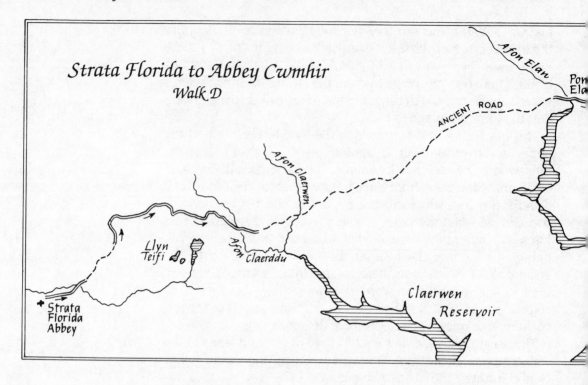

Strata Florida to Abbey Cwmhir
Walk D

Afon Elan

Pon
Ela

ANCIENT ROAD

Afon Claerwen

Llyn
Teifi

Afon Claerddu

Claerwen
Reservoir

+ Strata
Florida
Abbey

clung to many of the customs of the first Celtic church, a matter which Gerald found deeply disturbing:

> *It is remarkable that this church, like many others in Wales and Ireland, has a lay abbot, for a bad custom has prevailed amongst the clergy of appointing the most powerful people of a parish stewards or rather patrons of their churches . . . Such defenders, or rather destroyers, of the church, have caused themselves to be called abbots, and presumed to attribute to themselves a title, as well as estates to which they have no just claim. In this state we found the church of Llanpadarn, without a head. A certain old man, waxen old in iniquity, being abbot and his sons officiating at the altar . . . This wicked people boast, that a certain bishop of their church*

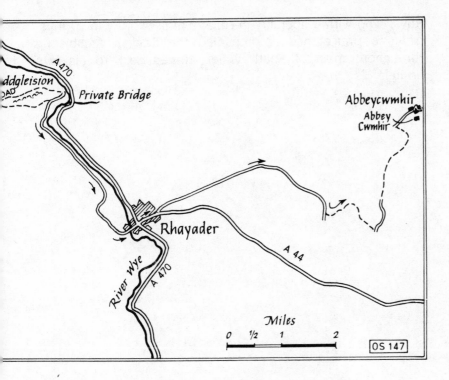

(for it formerly was a cathedral) was murdered by their
predecessors: and on this account, chiefly, they ground
their claims of right and possession. No public complaint having been made against their conduct, we have
thought it more prudent to pass over, for the present, the
enormities of this wicked race with dissimulation, than
exasperate them by a further narration.

Notwithstanding the compromise they had to make with such
wickedness, Gerald, and the probably more tolerant Baldwin,
spent a night with the community at Llanbadarn Fawr, attracting
'many persons to the service of Christ on the following morning'.
They then set out towards the mountainous, sea-girt wilderness
of North Wales, which they entered after they had made the
crossing of the Dovey. On the southern bank of that river, Lord

Rhys, 'who with a liberality peculiarly praiseworthy in so illustrious a prince' had accompanied the English Archbishop throughout most of South Wales, turned back to his own homelands.

CHAPTER SEVEN

The Mountains of the North

Going north from Llanbadarn Fawr, the Archbishop crossed the Dovey by boat, and then made for Tywyn, where the Augustinian priests, who served the church of St Cadfan, had invited him to spend the night. The sands of the Dovey estuary have shifted to such an extent through the centuries, that it is not possible to be completely clear as to where a river crossing would have been made in 1188. A causeway goes down to the water a little to the east of Aberdovey, and if the tradition that the Romans paved that path were true, then this could well have been the place where Baldwin landed. Unfortunately for that theory, the truth of the matter is that the slipway was built by French prisoners of war, taken in the Napoleonic Wars.

The Dovey Estuary

Nowadays, although it is possible to take a ferry from Aberdovey from the dunes of Twyni Bâch (612944), most people journey north through Machynlleth, and then make for the coast by the road which first came into being in 1827. The older road, turnpiked in 1775, goes into the hills from the village of Cwrt, and that is still the most interesting way to approach Tywyn.

The walk to Tywyn leaves the old road from Cwrt just before it enters the Happy Valley and meets the streams which feed the Bearded Lake (653988), so called for the mass of reeds and rushes that grow there. From that point an old drove road climbs north-west through rocky outcrops to reach the high valley along which the Nant Braich-y-rhiw flows to join the Dysynni. This path widens to join the lane going down to Rhyd-yr-onen; but it is pleasanter to cross the stream, and take the grassy path following the contours of the hill above a little wood and then turning to the earthworks by the farm of Bryn-y-castell (614018)

Walk A: Cwrt to Tywyn (OS sheet 135)

and from there to make for the narrow gauge Talyllyn Railway, laid down in 1866 to take the slate from the quarries round Cadair Idris to the coast. The walker must leave the track at Croes-faen and join the A 493, a mile to the east of Tywyn.

Tywyn

Tywyn is a holiday town with an oddly spacious Victorian air about it, largely due to its unrealised ambition to become a successful spa, after its estate was sold in 1874 to John Corbett, who had established Droitwich as a fashionable place to take the waters. He hoped that Tywyn's iron-rich well would prove equally

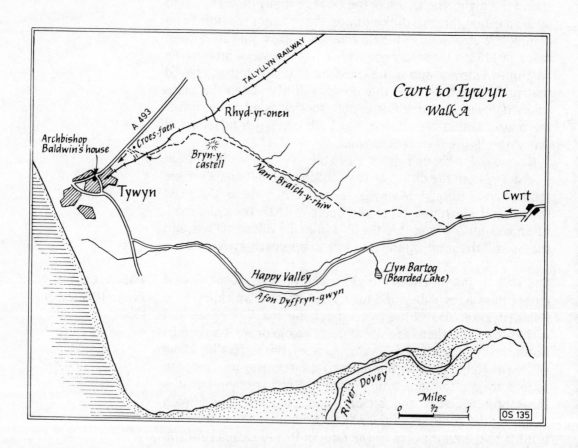

beneficial for the wealth of the Welsh town, and for the health of those with money enough to come here for the cure. It was not to happen. However the solid public buildings, which were put up in expectation of the wealthy visitors, remain.

So, more interestingly, does the twelfth-century church, whose shrine to the sixth-century Breton saint, Cadfan, really did draw crowds of pilgrims across the mountains throughout the middle ages. Naturally the well, where miraculous cures were then said to take place in the saint's name, provided the waters for Corbett's spa.

The abbey in which Baldwin stayed has disappeared, but tradition has it that it stood close to the present vicarage. A three-storey dwelling on that site, known as Archbishop Baldwin's House, was demolished in 1960 to make way for a new housing development. However one wall of an older building still remains, marked by wooden and slate lintels above in-filled doors and windows. They are certainly much later than the twelfth century, but may actually mark the place of the Archbishop's lodging.

From there it is a short walk to the church, served by Augustinian canons from 950, and built about a hundred years before Baldwin's visit. The nave and sanctuary still date from that time, but the tower which Baldwin saw collapsed in 1692, and the present one dates from the time of Corbett's rebuilding. One ancient memorial stone within the church is of peculiar interest for it carries the earliest written Welsh on record. The importance of this stone and its inscription was long unrecognised. For years it stood out in the weather, serving as a way-marker on the Aberdovey road.

Gerald says nothing of the route that was taken from Tywyn to the next serious river crossing at the Mawddach, when the Archbishop set out accompanied by Gruffydd ap Cynan, a princeling of Gwynedd. He had arrived in Tywyn early in the morning of Baldwin's departure, 'humbly and devoutly asking pardon for having so long delayed his attention to the Archbishop'. It would indeed have been more courteous, if he had welcomed the prelate on the north shore of the Dovey; and his grovelling apologies were much in order, for other men had been threatened with excommunication for such tardiness. It is a pity that Gerald does not record what excuses he offered, for this Gruffydd seems to have been a man of great religious feeling. When he died twelve years later, he was buried in Bangor cathedral in the cowl of a monk.

Birds Rock (OS *sheet* 124)

Gerald probably made no reference to the route along which the cavalcade rode north from Tywyn because it followed a track so well-known as the pilgrim way from the east to St Cadfan's shrine, that it seemed to him to be superfluous to comment on it. It is not so straightforward a matter now, again because of the shifting coastline, to trace the way that they reached the mountain track from the vast, swampy marsh that lay to the north of Tywyn. An indication of how far the sea has receeded is given by the remarkable Birds Rock, five miles inland in the Dysynni valley (643065). On the narrow, precipitous ledges of this wedge-shaped outcrop, twenty pairs of cormorants have nested for generations. Nowhere else in Britain do these seabirds fly so far inland at sunset. In the late eighteenth century the land of this wide valley was drained and crops were grown on land that was probably underwater when Baldwin made his journey.

Llangelynn

The modern traveller returns to the world that would be more familiar to twelfth-century eyes at the tiny coastal church of Llangelynn (572071), where St Celynn, to whom the church is dedicated, settled his llan sometime in the late seventh century. Obviously nothing is left of that original church, which was probably built of wood, but the present stone building, inevitably much-restored over the years, was there when Baldwin rode into the mountains above it. Although the porch was renovated in 1884, its simple rough stonework and slate slabs are as timeless as the flags that form the floor of the tiny nave. Its most remarkable trophy is a bier, hung on the north wall. It is unique of its kind for it has horse shafts at either end, a reminder of the time when two horses, providing a pull-and-push drive, were

needed to negotiate the steep slopes from the mountain farms
to the coastal burial plot.

The walker gets a better understanding of these funeral problems
by going inland and tackling the steep lanes which climb above
the Dysynni valley. Indeed the way to reach the old mountain
road is to go into the hills from Llanegryn and so up to the farm
buildings of Cae'rmynach, whence a track winds higher up the
western slopes of Alt-lwyd and then descends to the cwm, where
the narrow Dyffryn is flanked by terraces of long-deserted and
almost completely crumbled mine-workings. This stretch of track
through the valley is traditionally said to be on the site of a
Roman road, and certainly there is clear evidence all around that
this way was used by early travellers long before the age of the
saints turned it into a pilgrim route. In the forestry ground to the
west of the path, there is a massive stone barrow, one of many
prehistoric sites, that show traces of settlement here.

Back on open ground again, beneath the rocks of Craig Cwm-
llwyd, it is possible to look west across the sea to the outline of
the Lleyn peninsula and the looming shape of Bardsey Island.
Gerald was properly fascinated by that sacred place, inhabited by
the Culdees, inheritors of that Celtic church which drew from him
such strong and ambivalent feelings. However, there is no doubt
where his sympathies lay when he wrote:

> This island, either from the wholesomeness of its climate,
> owing to its vicinity to Ireland, or rather from some
> miracle obtained by the merits of the saints, has this
> wonderful peculiarity, that the oldest people die first,
> because diseases are uncommon, and scarcely any die
> except from extreme old age . . . very many bodies of
> saints are said to be buried there, amongst them that of
> Daniel, bishop of Bangor.

Bardsey Island is a long way from this walk over the broad
shoulder of Cadair Idris, yet although Baldwin's journey would
take him closer to it, he would never again have the chance to see

**Walk B: Llanegryn
to Arthog**

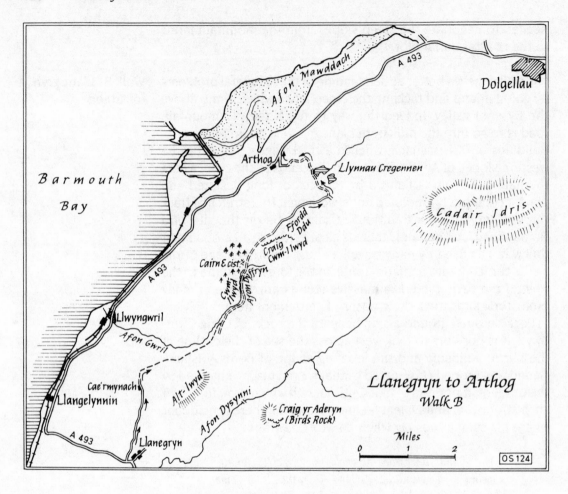

Llanegryn to Arthog
Walk B

it so clearly. It would be lost to view as he reached the twin lakes of Llynnau Cregenen and the rugged descent, which now comes out at the main road near the neat little village of Arthog, by the salt marshes of the Mawddach.

Gerald, who described that river as being 'bifurcate' probably intended his readers to understand that Baldwin made the crossing at its confluence with the Wnion which flows somewhat to the east of their route. However, Lord Rhys's son Malgon (still clearly intending to honour his commitment to the crusade) was more impatient to get to the north and found 'a ford near the sea'. The present road bridge from Dolgellau crosses the Wnion at some distance from the Mawddach crossing. The Archbishop's party, however, were ferried over both waters, which may well have been much wider than they are today.

Cymmer Abbey

The present road bridge crosses to the A 496. At 717189 a lane comes out and goes directly north, by the ruins of Cymmer Abbey, founded as a Cistercian settlement in 1198 by monks from Abbey Cwmhir, a venture that was made possible by the support of that same Gruffydd ap Cynan who came so tardily to Tywyn. Although the remains of this smallest of Welsh monasteries stand close to a farm whose main crop is caravans, the glade in which the white monks lived and worked is still a peaceful place. Sheep graze among the stones that trace cloister and frater, and trees screen the pillars of the abbey church from the more garish intrusions of the modern world.

Walk C: Bontddu to Llanbedr

The next part of the way, which goes through the Rhinogs and Ardudwy, enters an area that is truly remote, and in which, even in high summer, it is still possible to walk alone. Baldwin may well have struck out to the north from the present village of Bontddu (673187), whose gold mines, which reached a peak of production in the late 1860s, still provide material for royal wedding rings. This place also stands on the route taken by the London to Harlech coach in the eighteenth century. That four-in-hand climbed up to the northern ridge, before descending to cross the astoundingly narrow Pont-Scethin, which still bridges the Ysgethin between the two lakes of Irddyn and Bodlyn.

It is most likely that Baldwin's cavalcade of carts and tumbrils would not have gone north to Pont-Scethin, but have turned west here to the pass of Bwlch y Rhiwgyr, a way used for centuries by the Harlech drovers. However anyone who has followed Gerald thus far must want to see more of the Rhinogs, which he described as 'the rudest and roughest district of all Wales; the ridges of its mountains are very high and narrow, terminating in sharp peaks, and so irregularly jumbled together, that if the shepherds conversing or disputing with each other, from their summits, should agree to meet, they could scarcely effect their purpose in the course of the whole day.'

In order to test the truth of his observations, it is necessary to stay on the old Harlech road, as it winds down to the isolated, steep arch of Pont-Scethin, and then climb north to Cwm Nantcol. Here the way goes past the stones and grassy humps which mark the remains of an old coaching inn, strangely close to its journey's end.

Cwm Nantcol ends at the foot of a steep pass, whose lower slopes are covered in whortle berries. Conifers clothe the hills to the east of it, so once across the mountain, the way goes partly through forestry paths before coming to the more famous crossing of the Rhinogs which leads to the Roman steps. On a clear day, it is well worthwhile pausing after the climb, before making the final descent, in order to clamber out to the further cairn of the two to the north. From that vantage point it is possible to look out across the wide stretches of sandy marsh that stretch between Harlech and Porthmadog; and to try to imagine what it must have been like before the nineteenth-century draining of the coastal lowland, into which the Glaslyn river, swollen by the waters of the Snowdon range, flows and spreads. William Maddocks' engineers, who were responsible for that massive feat in 1820, altered the lie of the land so substantially that it is impossible now to make any accurate trace of the route that Baldwin must have taken on his way to Lleyn.

The stone slabs that mark the path on the western side of this pass, running between bare, forbidding black rock, present much less uncertainty. This carefully made way follows the only possible route, but the series of steps, which help the traveller, were probably not engineered by the Romans as popular belief would have it. It is now thought that it is more likely that this way was paved and drained in order to facilitate a much used packhorse trade route from the middle ages. It only serves

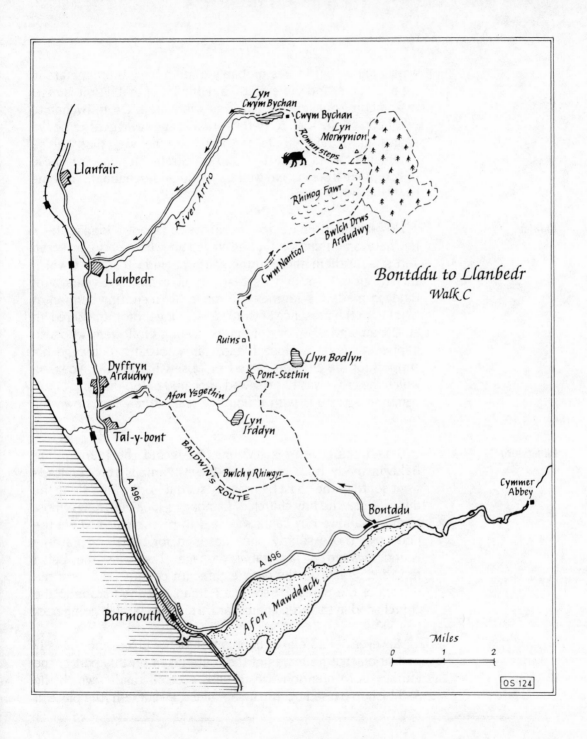

Lyn
Cwym Bychan

Cwym Bychan

Lyn
Morwynion

Roman steps

Rhinog Fawr

Bwlch Drws
Arddwy

River Arrio

Llanfair

Cwm Nantcol

Llanbedr

Bontddu to Llanbedr
Walk C

Ruins

Llyn Bodlyn

Pont-Scethin

Dyffryn
Arddwy

Afon Ysgethin

Llyn
Irddyn

Tal-y-bont

BALDWIN'S ROUTE

Bwlch y Rhiwgyr

Cymmer
Abbey

Bontddu

A 496

A 496

Afon Mawddach

Barmouth

Miles

0   1   2

OS 124

walkers now, but is was probably quite a busy thoroughfare in Gerald's time, and there is still a reminder of that. For it is here, or sometimes beside the lane that winds from Cwym Bychan to Llanbedr, on the road to Harlech, that shaggy wild goats crop the sparse grass and nibble the trees, in the way that Leland complained their ancestors did at Strata Florida. For these unkempt creatures could well be the feral descendants of some twelfth-century herd.

Llanfair

However Baldwin got to Llanfair, he had made a long journey, for there is no mention that he stayed anywhere between Tywyn and this northern shore to the south of Harlech, a place which was to grow up round its castle built a hundred years after Baldwin made his journey. He made his recruiting sermon at Llanfair in the presence of Gruffydd's younger brother, Meredyth ap Conan; and when one of that princeling's followers, who also happened to be a close friend, came forward to pledge his support for the crusade, Meredyth 'observing that the cloak, on which the cross was to be sewed appeared of too thin and of too common a texture, with a flood of tears, threw him down his own'.

Llandanwg

Gerald spared only a few lines to record the journey that Baldwin made from Llanfair to Lleyn. Perhaps the cavalcade went south to the coast before they set out northwards along the dunes. Here, the tiny church of Llandanwg (568283), now almost totally swallowed by sand, was said to be the place where the bodies of those saintly ones destined for burial on Bardsey Island awaited a favourable passage. That was the belief recorded as late as the early eighteenth century by one of the rectors of the parish. There is a Roman inscribed stone in the church, and in the little churchyard, a slate grave slab going back to 1600.

However Gerald makes no mention of the place, and the only indication that he leaves of the route taken on this part of the journey is to mention two recently erected castles which the Archbishop passed by. The first of these, Deudraeth (the place of

two sands) is easily located. It is on the Portmeirion peninsula –
not the Castelldeudraeth inscribed on the Ordnance Survey map.
This is a rather portentous nineteenth-century mansion now
serving as a restaurant for the enthusiasts who enjoy Clough
Williams Ellis's architectural, Italianate fantasy, which is surmounted by the motte of the castle (588372) which Gerald knew,
hidden in the trees above the holiday stage-set. Carn Madryn, the
second castle that Gerald mentions, is on Lleyn itself and can be
traced on the cliffs above Dinas (123: 496376).

Criccieth Castle which was to replace or augment Carn Madryn   *Criccieth (OS sheet*
fortification was to be built by the princes of Gwynedd in the   *123)*
thirteenth century. So it is unlikely that Gerald ever saw it.
However in 1188 his journey took him past the rocky promontory
on which it was to stand. From there he rode with Baldwin across
Lleyn to Nefyn, taking the route dictated by the lie of the land
from Chwilog to Rhyd-y-gwystl, a crossroads whose prehistoric
importance is emphasised by a standing stone and a bronze-age
burial chamber. Much later this place was to be used as a
collecting station for the black cattle who were driven out of this
peninsula to the English grazing grounds and eventually to
Smithfield. By the eighteenth century some three thousand of
them were to make that journey each year, supplying beef to the
English, while the people of Lleyn lived on oats and herring.

The way to the north-west from Rhyd-y-gwystl goes past   *Nefyn*
further standing stones, and then by the hill fort of Garn Boduan,
which rises above the coastal village of Nefyn, where the
Archbishop was to spend the eve of Palm Sunday. The following
day he embarked on Holy Week by preaching there and inducing
many people to take the cross. There is nothing in this holiday
place now to indicate where he either slept or spoke, and Gerald
was far too interested in his own personal success at the place to
make any record of where Baldwin stayed. For it was here that
'the archdeacon, after long enquiry and research, is said to have
found Merlin Sylvestris'.

It is a cryptic note, but an appropriate one, for Nefyn seems to have been strongly connected with the story of Arthur and the twelfth-century belief, fostered in Wales, that the fabled king would soon return to liberate his countrymen. Edward I was to scotch that when he held a dance and tournament at Nefyn and staged it in the manner of Arthur's Round Table, indicating that he was the monarch the Welsh were looking for. In 1188, however, it was still propitious that Gerald should find a trace of the wild Druid, Merlin Sylvestris, in this place.

He obviously believed there were two Merlins: Merlin Ambrosius and this Merlin Sylvestris or Celidonius of Arthur's Court, the half-crazed man, who lived some several hundred years after his more courtly namesake. According to Gerald they both 'foretold the destruction of their nation, as well as the coming of the Saxons, and afterwards that of the Normans'; a state of affairs that would be righted in due course when 'even the name of foreigners, shall be extinguished in the island, and the Britons shall exult again in their ancient name and privileges'.

Pistyll

Although Gerald makes no reference to Pistyll, it clearly lay on the Archbishop's route to the east. Its church is of far more absorbing interest to the historically (and romantically) minded visitor than anything that Nefyn can offer. This little twelfth-century building, dedicated to St Beuno (the David of the north) shelters in a hollow by the sea. It is an unusual and much loved place, quite apart from its antiquity, for here the traditions of the early Celtic church have been carefully melded with the old druidic festivals (such as the August celebration of Lammas) in a way that confirms and reveres the natural as well as the supernatural world.

Walk D: Pistyll to Llanaelhaearn

In the early middle ages there was a small Cistercian community here offering hospitality to those pilgrims whose route to Bardsey Island brought them to Pistyll from Llanaelhaearn, and the site of St Beuno's own llan at Clynnog-fawr. Part of the way that those pilgrims travelled can be followed from St Beuno's church at Pistyll over the hills to Gwylfa, and from that village by the pass at Bwlch to the clearing by a piece of forestry land to the

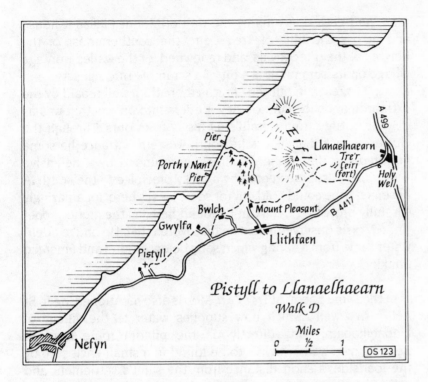

Pistyll to Llanaelhaearn
Walk D

north of Llithfaen. Through these trees a steep and stoney track winds down to the abandoned, quarry-encircled coastal village of Nant. No cars, other than those strictly engaged on official business, are allowed on that rough road. Indeed before it was built, the place was only accessible by sea, and two piers were constructed to enable the stone from the quarries to be shipped away. Now, the neatened terraces of the quarrymen's cottages have been transformed into a Welsh language school, where students can be immersed in the tongue away from any distractions of more familiar speech. Just above the shore are the few traces of the earlier occupation – rusting remains of railway lines and winches used until the workings were abandoned twenty-five years ago.

The way to the east continues to Llanaelhaearn along the

moorland path that runs by the wall of Mount Pleasant house and across the hills of Tre'r Ceiri, the southernmost of the heights of the three Rivals, and renowned for the walled iron-age village on its summit. It is a bit of a scramble through scree and heather to reach it, but the effort is more than well repaid by the extraordinary backward journey it offers into an age that was as distant in time from Gerald's as his is from ours. Through the clutter of rock that blocks its south-western entrance lie some hundred-and-fifty stone dwellings, surrounded by a defensive wall which is supplemented by a rocky precipice to the south. A beseiged tribe could hold out for some weeks here, for amazingly carefully protected wells can be found here, as the modern poet Brian Morris observed, when he discovered that 'Up on Tre'r Ceiri water came from a spring which sang below ground and emerged blinking'.

Clynnog-fawr (OS sheet 115)

In the same poem, *At Tre'r Ceiri*, Morris also mentioned 'deep St Aelhaern's well', which now supplies water to the village of Llanaelhaearn, lying directly on the pilgrim route from St Beuno's own well, which is to be found in a small enclosure by the roadside, a short distance from the saint's settlement and college at Clynnog-fawr. According to a tradition, endorsed by Leland, Beuno was buried in the chapel which is joined to the main body of the remarkably large church in that small village by an ancient covered passage. In that chapel, there is a stone, whose incised cross is said to have been marked out by the saint's thumb. It testifies to a grant of land, which the Welsh king, Cadwallon, granted to the holy man, thereby enabling him to settle on this narrow coastal plain.

Caernarfon

For years that stone stood just outside Caernarfon at the crossing of the River Seiont, and it is possible that Baldwin and Gerald rode by it as they entered that town, which had grown around the Roman fort of Segontium. However Gerald is reticent about this place, merely treating his readers to a lecture on the etymology of its name, in the course of which he at least acknowledges the presence of the castle, established in 1090 by

Hugh of Avranches, the first Norman lord of Chester. He may also have seen, although he makes no mention of it, the church of Llanbelig on the outskirts of the Roman settlement and dedicated to one of the sons of the Emperor Magnus Maximus, the Maxen of the *Mabinogion* and husband of the Helen who gave her name to the longest and best known of the Roman roads of Wales.

Somewhere to the east of Caernarfon, when the entourage came to a road leading to a steep valley:

> *we dismounted from our horses, and proceeded on foot, rehearsing as it were, by agreement, some experiments of our intended pilgrimage to Jerusalem. Having traversed the valley, and reached the opposite side with considerable fatigue, the Archbishop, to rest himself and recover his breath, sat down on an oak which had been torn up by the violence of the winds; and relaxing into a pleasantry, highly laudable in a person of his approved gravity, thus addressed his attendants: 'Who amongst you, in this company, can now delight our wearied ears by whistling?' which is not easily done by people out of breath.*

It is a delightful anecdote, but it is not so simple to say where it actually took place. After searching both the old and the new roads between Caernarfon and Bangor, Colt Hoare's early twentieth-century editor, W. Llewelyn Williams, finally settled for the Nant-y-Garth, in the grounds of Vaynol Hall, the home of a Mr Assheton-Smith, the nineteenth-century owner of the Dinorwic slate quarries at Llanberis. So now, the coastal path through the woods to the north of Port Dinorwic (526677) is generally taken to be the one stretch of his journey which Baldwin covered on foot.

He was to spend two nights at Bangor, where he and Gerald   *Bangor*
were 'well-entertained' by Bishop Guianus. That man was so beloved by his flock, that when, after Mass on the first morning of

the arch-episcopal visit, he felt compelled to take the cross 'at the insistence of the Archbishop and other persons more importunate than persuasive . . . all his people, of both sexes, expressed their grief on this occasion by loud and lamentable vociferations'.

Anglesey

That was an awkward start to a day which was to prove increasingly difficult, as Baldwin crossed the Menai straits, together with Seisyll, abbot of Strata Florida and Alexander, Archdeacon of Bangor, who was to act as the interpreter to the Welsh-speaking people for the remainder of the journey. As soon as Baldwin landed on Anglesey's shore, he was greeted by its princeling, Rhodri ap Owen and a great crowd of people. Confession was heard 'in a place near the shore, where the surrounding rocks seemed to form a natural theatre'. Then the three clerics preached, and 'many persons were induced to take the cross'. Despite that successful eloquence,

> *Many chosen youths of the family of Rhodri were seated on an opposite rock, and not one of them could be prevailed upon to take the cross, although the archbishop and others most earnestly exhorted them, but in vain, by an address particularly directed to them. It came to pass within three days, as if by divine vengeance, that these young men, with many others, pursued some robbers of that country. Being discomfited and put to flight, some were slain, others mortally wounded, the survivors voluntarily assumed that cross they had before despised.*

The place where the Archbishop and his accompanying prelates preached has now been totally obscured by the buildings around Telford's Menai Bridge. Only the shore around the tiny fifteenth-century church of St Tysilio (552716), on a little island that can only be reached by a footbridge, is left to remind the visitor of the empty place where the recalcitrant youths held out against Baldwin's preaching.

Although the Archbishop spent such a little time in Anglesey, Gerald was not deterred from devoting the best part of a chapter to the folklore of this fertile island. He makes a serious report of a stone that could move of its own volition; of a hill that produced some supernaturally extraordinary acoustic effects; and he appends yet another example to prove that divine retribution follows those who kennel dogs in a church. In this instance, the hounds ran mad, and their owner, the Earl of Shrewsbury, died within a month.

The best story, however, concerns the virtually inaccessible, holy island of Priestholm,

Priestholm

> *almost adjoining to Anglesey, which is inhabited by hermits, living by manual labour, and serving God. It is remarkable that when, by the influence of human passions, any discord arises among them, all their provisions are devoured and infected by a species of small mice, with which the island abounds: but when the discord ceases, they are no longer molested.*

This island lies offshore from the site of the thirteenth-century Augustinian priory of St Penmon, set up on the site of a Christian Celtic foundation, whose holy well and hermitage, where Anglesey's sixth-century Saint Seriol spent long, solitary hours of prayer, still retain something of the secluded peace with which the holy man imbued the place. For as Gerald noted, even in his day, 'hermits and anchorites more strictly abstinent and more spiritual can nowhere be found' than in Wales, a nation, 'earnest in all its pursuits'.

Gerald's stories of Anglesey are matched by those in a subsequent chapter, devoted to the legends of the Snowdon ranges, which the Archbishop had no reason to penetrate, although he may well have looked at the panorama of those mountains, and perhaps drawn strength from it, as he argued with the youths on the Anglesey shore.
    'The mountains of Eyri [Snowdon] could supply pasturage for

all the herds of cattle in Wales,' wrote Gerald, long before the rocks of those mountains had been torn apart by the slate quarries. And even his cherished Merlin could never have predicted that when that industry had come and gone the mountain paths would start to erode under the tread of hordes of walkers and climbers. Gerald's fantastic stories of the two mountain lakes would seem less incredible to twelfth-century readers than the changes that have in fact taken place here. They would have found no difficulty in accepting that there was one stretch of water noted for its floating island, blown from shore to shore by the wind; or that there was another inhabited by eels, trout and perch, none of which had any trace of a right eye. However Gerald was forced to confess that 'if the curious reader should demand the explanation of so extraordinary a circumstance, I cannot presume to satisfy him'.

'Vulgar tradition' had also informed him of 'an eagle who, perching on a fatal stone every fifth holiday, in order to satiate her hunger with the carcasses of the slain, is said to expect war on that same day, and to have almost perforated the stone by cleaning and sharpening her beak.' That may sound a bit like Edgar Allan Poe's raven or Lewis Carrol's 'monstrous crow' to us, but it was not the doom-laden bird, but Merlin, who really fascinated Gerald. So he could not forbear to write of the hill-fort of Dinas Emrys near Beddgelert, although he probably never climbed up to that remote and now inaccessible fastness to the west of Llyn Dinas, where Merlin Ambrosius uttered his prophecies to Vortigern.

That was all a marvellous diversion from the actual troubles in Bangor, for no sooner had Baldwin returned to Bangor cathedral from Anglesey, than he was shown 'the tombs of prince Owain and his younger brother Cadwalader, who were buried in a double vault before the high altar, although Owain, on account of his public incest with his cousin-german, had died excommunicated by the blessed martyr, St Thomas, the bishop of that see having been enjoined to seize a proper opportunity of removing his body from the church'.

Owain Gwynnedd had been in his tomb twelve years, when Baldwin, no doubt eagerly abbetted by Gerald, forced the wretched Guianus to remove his body to the churchyard. This sanctimonious horror of remote incest was naturally encouraged by the Normans, who wanted to break up the powerful Welsh dynasties. It was a campaign that Gerald (whose own blood was mixed) wholeheartedly supported, bewailing the inherent and deplorable predisposition of the Welsh to

> the crime of incest . . . that, not having the fear of God before their eyes, they are not ashamed of intermarrying with their relations, even in the third degree of consanguinity. They generally abuse these dispensations with a view of appeasing those enmities which so often subsist between them, because 'their feet are swift to shed blood'; and from their love of high descent, which they so ardently affect and covet, they unite themselves to their own people, refusing to intermarry with strangers, and arrogantly presuming on their own superiority of blood and family.

Having cleared the cathedral of Bangor from its unwelcome guest, the Archbishop and his entourage continued on their way to the east, taking a route 'confined on one side by steep rocks, and by the sea on the other'. Now that way is completely obscured by the massive, and seemingly continuous roadworks of the A 55, and there is no peace to be had in it. However there is an older route from Bangor to the east, and although Baldwin did not take it, this is now by far the best way to reach the west bank of the River Conwy, and from many parts of it, it is possible to have a full overview of the coastline and this part of Baldwin's journey.

It is a walk that leads some miles away from the noise of twentieth-century traffic, and which goes much further away in time, back beyond Gerald, past the Romans who laid the road on this track leading from their Chester to their Caernarfon and the

Walk E: Aber to the River Conwy

iron-age settlers of the hill-forts near to the cairns that mark the bronze-age ridgeway route. It is well to join it from the village of Aber (654726) and to cross the Afon Rhaeadr-fawr (the river of the great waterfall) at Bont Newydd (the new bridge built in the early nineteenth century at the place of an often-flooded ford). Before following the track to the east, however, those who cannot resist a good waterfall will be well repaid by taking a diversion through the woods to the south to Aber Falls where the water tumbles magnificently over the rocks and so gives the river its name.

From Bont Newydd, the Roman road climbs over Bwlch y Ddeufaen, the pass of the two stones. These are prehistoric standing stones, some six foot high, and they mark the route, which was much travelled long before the Romans came. Some three miles further to the east there is an even more impressive reminder of the early men who walked and settled here. This is

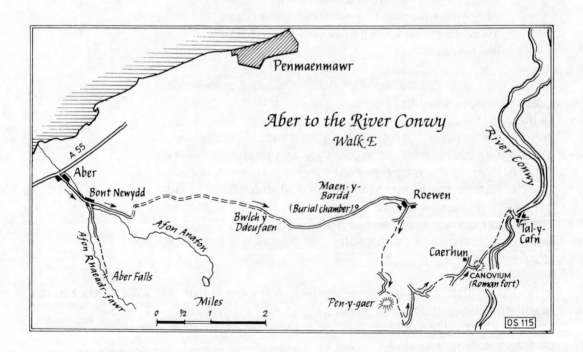

the great megalithic cyst of Maen-y-Bardd (the Bard's stone). From its great stones, a lane leads to the neat little village of Roewen, and from there it is well worthwhile making another diversion to the south before visiting the Roman fort of Cano-vium on the fertile Conwy plain.

This diversion leads to the iron-age hill-fort of Pen-y-gaer, which is remarkable in having an additional outer defence in the shape of a stretch of sloping ground set with a mass of pointed stones, dragons' teeth, which would seriously slow down any mounted, invading hordes intent on scaling the double ramparts of the settlement. From that hill top, lanes lead down to the village of Caerhun and the site of the Roman camp of Canovium from which a footpath follows the river north to the site of the Roman crossing of the Conwy at Tal-y-Cafn.

Conwy

Baldwin's entrance into Conwy took him past the Cistercian abbey founded three years previously, and to be moved up river to Maenan (791658) a hundred years later, when Edward I wanted to consolidate his victory over the Welsh by building a magnificent fortification by the Conwy estuary to replace the more modest castle of Deganwy (784797). Thousands of visitors each year flock to Conwy castle, but few know of its predecessor, standing above a spacious suburb of Conwy town. Two fields separate the houses from the grassy earthworks which indicate this stronghold of dark age princes on which the Normans built their first defence of the river.

Rhuddlan (OS sheet 116)

The Archbishop was bound further east, for he was to spend the night at Rhuddlan, being 'handsomely entertained' at the 'noble castle' belonging to no less a person than the son and offspring of the 'incestuous marriage' contracted by that Owain Gwynnedd, who had been so ignominiously despatched from Bangor cathedral. The motte of his castle, now written of as 'Twt Hill', stood up-river from the site where Edward I was to build his own magnificent fortification, whose towers still overshadow the water.

A hundred years before the Archbishop's visit, the Norman

Robert of Rhuddlan established a mint here, and pennies were still being coined from the local silver mines, commented upon by Gerald, until the thirteenth century. So Rhuddlan was an important place, and one in which Baldwin was able to persuade many people 'to dedicate themselves to the service of Christ'. After that achievement, the cavalcade rode south along the banks of the Clywd to St Asaph, the last of the four Welsh cathedrals in which Baldwin was to preach.

St Asaph   This cathedral is built on the site where the sixth-century Kentigern, of whom St Asaph was a disciple, is said to have established a large monastic community during his exile from north Britain. The building in which Baldwin preached has disappeared, for it was burnt down by Edward I's soldiers in 1282. The present cathedral's chief memorial is to the sixteenth-century bishop, William Morgan, who produced the first transla-tion of the Bible into Welsh. That serves as its greatest historical interest, for as the nineteenth-century Catholic poet, Gerard Manley Hopkins, observed, the fabric of St Asaph was so heavily restored in his time that most of its earlier structure has been overlaid.

The Jesuit college of St Beuno, where Hopkins lived from 1874 to 1877, and where he learnt the Welsh that was to have such an influence on the sprung-rhythms of his own verse, stands at the northern edge of the Clwyd range, above the village of Tremeir-chion (083732). From there the road runs east to Holywell, which the Archbishop must have passed by, but which Gerald oddly saw fit to ignore.

Holywell   This holy well of St Winefride is the British Lourdes, and still attracts hundreds of pilgrims who come to bathe in its waters. The tradition is that Winefride was a niece of St Beuno, and that she submitted to beheading rather than comply with the pagan prince who would have seduced her. According to William Caxton's printed life, in the very place where that virgin's head touched the ground there 'sprang up a weele of spryngyng water largely endurying to this day, which heleth al langours and sekenesses as well in men as in bestes, which welle is named after the name of the Vyrgyne and is called St Wenefrede's Well'.

Gerald must have known of these holy waters, for they had been a well-observed focus of pilgrimage long before he came here with Baldwin. In 1115, the Norman Earl Richard went 'devoutly to Holywell in pilgrimage for his great merite and gostly advantage'. In 1157, Henry II established a house of Knights Templars at nearby Basingwerk solely to protect the pilgrims to Holywell, and it was there that Baldwin was to spend his last night on Welsh soil. The ruins of Basingwerk Abbey, where Cistercian monks had lived alongside the Templars, now stands in a carefully, but unobtrusively, tended country park, which serves the industrial area of the Dee estuary, whose buildings seem more transitory than the yellow limestone of the abbey's crumbling walls.

Basingwerk Abbey

CHAPTER EIGHT

Through Shrewsbury to Hereford

Baldwin intended to celebrate Easter in Chester, so his stay in Basingwerk was brief. After one night's rest, they set out on the morning of Maundy Thursday to tackle the quicksands of the Dee estuary. After their previous experiences, Gerald was not ashamed to confess that they viewed this prospect with some apprehension. Once again it is not possible to be sure of the route that was taken or where the actual crossing of the river took place. Gerald noted that they went over the Dee, 'below Chester', and perhaps that was somewhere in the region of the modern Queensferry, a section of the river that has now been canalised. In the twelfth century the course of the Dee was so unpredictable that Gerald maintained that 'the inhabitants of these parts assert, that the waters of this river change their fords every month, and, as it inclines more towards England or Wales, they can with certainty, prognosticate which nation will be successful or unfortunate during the year'.

Chester (OS sheet 117)

It is a piece of folklore which gives a fair indication of the troubled border country that Baldwin had to ride through on his way to the south; but however he came to Chester, the modern visitor will do best to approach the city by the minor road (branching off the A 483) from Eccleston, which covers the Roman Watling Street and make the river crossing by the southern bridge. Chester is a place that lives in its history, and one that has long drawn tourists to revel in a stereotype 'Merrie England' which happily manages to leave the genuine impact of its ancient walls untouched. On public holidays stallholders dressed in various versions of medieval gear mingle among crowds eager for the more active excitement provided by the canoeists trying out their skills by the weir on the east bank of the river. In Gerald's time, Chester had another rare delicacy to offer her visitors. The Countess made cheeses out of deer's milk, a food that Gerald had not encountered elsewhere. He reported that Baldwin was presented with three examples of these novelties.

Although his tour of Wales was virtually at an end, and although Lent was over, the Archbishop was still mindful of his main task. In Chester, he celebrated Easter 'with due solemnity' and persuaded many more stalwart young men to take the cross; but there is no way of knowing whereabouts in the city it was that he delivered his sermon. If he had stayed at the Benedictine Abbey founded a hundred years previously on the site of the shrine of the seventh-century Saxon saint, Werburga, some mention might surely have been made in Gerald's account of Robert of Hastings, who was then the abbot. The Benedictine's church was to become the present cathedral in the year following the dissolution of the monastery, but subsequent extensive restoration has overlaid much of the pre-Reformation building. So it is much easier to imagine Baldwin preaching among the Norman arches of St John the Baptist's, the church which stands beside the site of Chester's Roman amphitheatre.

St John's Church

In 1075, St John's was built as the cathedral of West Mercia, an honour it was only to enjoy for ten years, for the see was soon established at Lichfield. St John's retained its importance however, and two years after Baldwin's visit it became a collegiate church. Whether or not it was here that the Archbishop celebrated Easter, Gerald was certainly well aware of the building and gave some credence to the tradition that Harold Godwinson actually survived Duke William's onslaught at Hastings and escaped to live out his days as an anchorite attached to St John's church in Chester.

Malpas

From Chester, Baldwin's entourage made for Oswestry, but in such a troubled area it was not wise to take the direct route, so the Archbishop was forced to skirt Powys, whose Welsh rulers were likely to have nothing but hostility for Henry II's envoy. This meant riding into Oswestry by way of Whitchurch, a route that took them south-east out of Chester, and probably along the Roman road running through the village of Malpas, where a border castle defended the surrounding rich farmlands from the Welsh raiders. Visitors are drawn here now by the elegant clerestory of the fourteenth century hill-top church, which replaces the building that once dominated this uneasy territory. In 1300 the inhabitants of Malpas were complaining that none of them dared to go to Mass on Easter day for fear of the marauding Welsh. These raids, however, were not solely responsible for the ill-starred name of the place. That probably is derived from *Malum Passum* (the bad way) an indication that in wet weather the old road could be virtually impassable.

Oswestry (OS *sheet* 126)

Without stopping at Whitchurch Abbey, Baldwin turned south-west to Oswestry, where he and Gerald 'were most sumptuously entertained after the English manner, by William Fitz Alan, a noble and liberal young man'. Once again this was no quiet and easy place. Twenty-three years before Baldwin's visit, when Henry II came here on an expedition into Powys, he was, as Gerald recalled

> *compelled by a sudden and violent fall of rain to retreat with his army. On the preceeding day, the chiefs of the English army had burned some of the Welsh churches, with the villages and churchyards; upon which the sons of Owain the Great, with their light-armed troops, stirred up the resentment of their father and the other princes of the country, declaring that they would never in future spare any churches of the English.*

Owain refused to concede to such blasphemous violence, arguing that by such barbarous actions as the English had committed, that nation must have lost the favour of 'divine assistance', and that the Welsh could further such an advantage if they would 'pay greater reverence than ever to churches and holy places'. It is ironic that this Owain, who spoke so wisely, was the very man whose body was thought to cause such sacrilege to the cathedral at Bangor. Indeed during the course of his visit to Oswestry, Baldwin put an end to another incestuous marriage in which Owain Gwynnedd was implicated through his daughter Angharad, who had become the wife of her cousin, Gruffydd ap Madog.

William Fitz Alan's castle is now in a sadly shoddy public park, a tump overgrown by a jungle of neglected, dingy shrubs and tangled grasses. The few remaining stones of the building that so delighted Gerald are protected by a cage-like structure at the top of the mound. It contrasts starkly with Oswestry's efficient, streamlined unadorned town hall across the street. Quite the most pleasing part of this ancient town now is centred round the spacious area surrounding the vast parish church, whose impressive early seventeenth-century tower is set on a wide Norman base. Nearby, on the site of the old defensive 'Welsh walls' there is a primary school which has been named for the English Fitz Alan.

Gerald noted that 'from Oswestry, we directed our course towards Shrewsbury', but made no reference to the route that the entourage took to the east. Still he infers that the Archbishop was in no hurry, for when they reached that city they were to remain there 'a few days to rest and refresh ourselves'. So it is possible that Baldwin might have been side-tracked from the direct way, and braved a visit across the border in order to visit the Cistercian abbey of Strata Marcella near the modern Welshpool. The community there would certainly be aware of the Archbishop's presence in Oswestry and would certainly have had mixed feelings about it.

All that is left of their abbey now is the glacial erratic said to have formed part of the abbot's throne, a massive boulder which has now been placed just outside the main door of St Mary's church in Welshpool; and a few stones on the actual site, founded in 1172, on the west bank of the Severn between Pool Quay and Buttington, some three miles to the north of Welsh-

Strata Marcella

pool. Here Owain Cyfelliog, Prince of South Powys, was to be buried in holy ground although he had been excommunicated by Baldwin for refusing to take the cross, or even to attend the Archbishop in Shrewsbury. Nevertheless when he died in 1197, the Third Crusade had already foundered, and the brothers concluded that God alone would judge the prince's decision. It was an attitude approved or at least tolerated by Gerald, for he visited the abbey in 1202 and preached to the community.

Some of the carved stones from Strata Marcella have found a resting place in the excellent little Powysland Museum, on the hill above St Mary's church. It also houses a copy of the earliest printed document in Wales, an indulgence issued by Strata Marcella's last abbot eight years before the Dissolution, and set up in type by a former apprentice of Caxton. Gerald would probably have been less cynical about the matter of indulgences and pardons than the sixteenth-century reformers. Early in his *Itinerary* he quoted a story about the repentance and pardon of Strata Marcella's first abbot, which he had learnt from Meilyr, the contemporary bard and prophet of Caerleon.

The fall of Enoch, abbot of Strata Marcella, too well known in Wales, was revealed to many the day after it happened, by Meilyr, who being asked how he knew this circumstance, said that a demon came to him disguised as a hunter, and, exulting in the prospect of such a victory, foretold the ruin of the abbot, and explained in what manner he would make him run away with a nun from the monastery. The end in view was probably the humiliation and correction of the abbot, as was proved from his shortly returning home, so humbled and amended, that he scarcely could be said to have erred.

Walk A: Over Breidden Hill

From Buttington, on the east bank of the Severn, it is possible to join a section of the officially designated Offa's Dyke Path, which links up with the remains of the actual earthwork to the south-west of Breidden Hill. From here a lane runs up to the quarry-scarred slopes, and to the footpath which leads through forestry

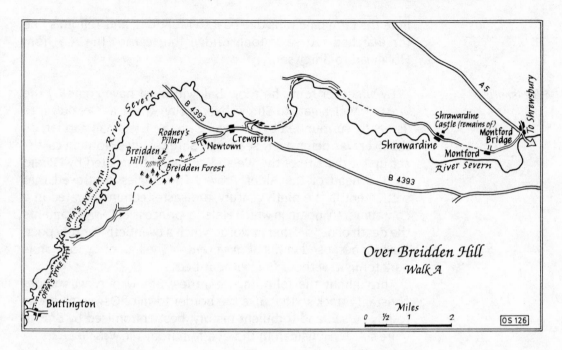

Over Breidden Hill

Walk A

Miles

0   ½   1   2

OS 126

land to the treeless summit, from which there is a fine view of the Severn plain to the east, and the scene of the turbulent border country, which Baldwin avoided as far as he was able.

On this height, a pillar commemorates Admiral Rodney's naval victory at Dominica in 1782, and unintentionally pays a sad tribute to the mature oaks of Shropshire, sacrificed to build his three-deckers. A few of their descendants still clothe the north-eastern hillside, rising above the villages of Newtown and Crewgreen and one of the few bridges across the meandering Severn.

The footpath comes out of the forest at Newtown and follows the lane through Crewgreen to the footpath going east through fields to the B 4393.

Across the bridge, a footpath runs by the riverside, heading in a generally easterly direction towards the remains of Shrawardine Castle, a border keep dismantled by the Roundheads in 1645, and existing now as a grassy earthwork by a farmyard. From here the farm lane runs due east to Montford, and Telford's fine three-arched red sandstone bridge that carries the A 5 from Holyhead to Shrewsbury.

Shrewsbury

By whatever route he took, Baldwin must have come by the West, or Welsh gate to Shrewsbury, a city, which, as Gerald wrote 'is nearly surrounded by the river Severn'. The small gap left by the river was defensively sealed by Shrewsbury's Norman castle, set up on the site of the Welsh Pengwern, translated by Gerald as 'the head of the Alder Grove'. The Angles destroyed that settlement in the ninth century, a disaster commemorated in a contemporary poem in which Heledd, princess of Powys, laments the death of her brother in words which a twentieth-century poet, David Jones, used in his *Sleeping Lord* – 'The hall of Cynddyian is dark tonight, without fire, without bed'.

Throughout the following centuries, Shrewsbury was under constant attack so that, like the border town of Oswestry, it was to have a sad and turbulent history, best epitomised by Shropshire's A. E. Housman in the quatrain from *The Welsh Marches*

> The flag of morn in conqueror's state
> Enters at the English gate:
> The vanquished eve, as night prevails,
> Bleeds upon the road to Wales.

The place was settled enough in 1188 for Baldwin to spend some days there, presumably staying in the castle, although Gerald makes no reference to their lodging. Both men preached in the city and 'many people were induced to take the cross, through the elegant sermons of the archbishop and the archdeacon'. Their other piece of business was to excommunicate Owain Cyfelliog, 'because he alone, amongst the Welsh princes, did not come to meet the archbishop with his people'. His disloyalty was strange, yet somehow in character, for as Gerald related, in the following anecdote, he was a man who had achieved an easy familiarity with Henry II.

> Owain was a man of more fluent speech than his contemporary princes, and was conspicuous for the good management of his territory. Having generally favoured the royal cause, and opposed the measures of his own chieftains, he had contracted a great familiarity with King Henry II. Being with the king at table at Shrewsbury, Henry, as a mark of peculiar honour and regard, sent him one of his own loaves; he immediately brake it into small pieces, like alms-bread, and having, like an almoner, placed them at a distance from him, he took them up one by one and ate them. The king requiring an explanation of this proceeding, Owain, with a smile replied, 'I thus follow the example of my lord', keenly alluding to the avaricious disposition of the king, who was accustomed to retain for a long time in his own hands the vacant ecclesiastical benefices.

That incident, which must have taken place sometime after Henry's disastrous expedition into Powys in 1165, demonstrates that Owain was certainly not a man to try and curry favour, an attitude that may well have led to his excommunication.

That business having been attended to, Baldwin and Gerald set out from Shrewsbury after a few days' rest. It was the last stage of their journey, and they were to travel back to Hereford by way of Wenlock, Bromfield, Ludlow and Leominster. They must surely have spent two days on the way, but Gerald makes no mention of the time they took, nor does he explain why, once again, they should have taken so zig-zag a route.

The only clue that he gives his readers is to tell the following anecdote about the way that they went:

> From Shrewsbury, we continued our journey towards Wenlock, by a narrow and rugged way, called Evil-Street, where in our time, a Jew, travelling with the archdeacon of the place, whose name was Sin (Peccatum), and the dean, whose name was Devil (De Eyville), towards Shrewsbury, hearing the archdeacon

say, that his archdeaconry began at a place called Evil-Street, and extended as far as Mal-pas, towards Chester, pleasantly told him, 'It would be a miracle, if his fate brought him safely out of a country, whose archdeacon was Sin, whose dean the devil; and the entrance to the archdeaconry Evil-Street, and its exit Bad-pass.

Malpas in Cheshire is quite unambiguous, but there are conflicting ideas about the Shropshire Evil Street (Malam plateam). It could refer to the Roman road, now the course of the A 49, which runs through the valley to the south of Shrewsbury, or to the ten-mile ridgeway track along the Long Mynd. In either case it is certain that the entourage did not go directly to Wenlock, by turning south-east from Shrewsbury. Whether it took the way along the valley or across the hills would have depended on the weather, for if there were heavy spring floods the low lying route may well have been impassable. There is no way of knowing. Gerald, as ever, makes no reference at all to the weather.

Walk B: The Long Mynd (OS sheet 137)

Although the Archbishop's route is in doubt, there is no question as to which is the pleasanter way today. The walk along the Long Mynd starts from the pretty village of Woolstaston, whose Victorian vicar, Edmund Donald Carr lost his way on the hills in January 1865, and spent twenty-seven hours wandering in the snow – Evil Street indeed.

That is not the whole character of the place. On a fine spring day it is pleasant to walk through the heather of this high moorland, intersected by deeply incised curving valleys and overlooking the 'Little Switzerland' around Church Stretton, a seemingly safe, picturesque scene, apart from some evil stretches of bog water along the way, which the Reverend Carr was fortunate enough not to fall into.

The way goes past the barrows known as Robin Hood's Butts, over Pole Bank, 1,500 feet and the highest point of the range, to the site of the Midland Gliding Club, a journey through time from

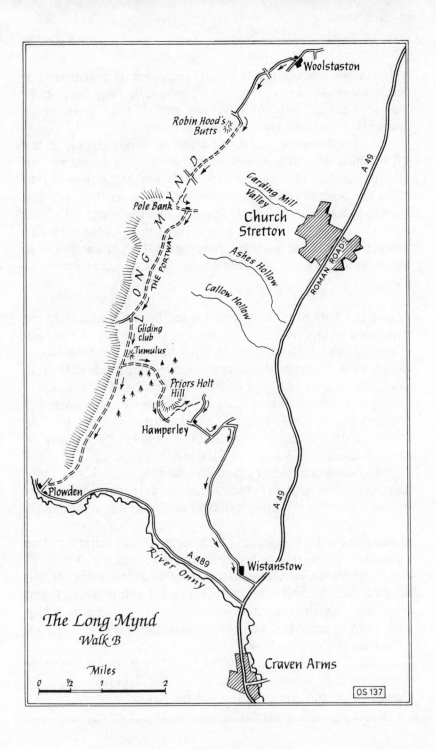

Woolstaston

Robin Hood's
Butts

L O N G   M Y N D

Carding Mill
Valley

A 49

Pole Bank

Church
Stretton

THE PORTWAY

Ashes Hollow

ROMAN ROAD

Callow Hollow

Gliding
club

Tumulus

Priors Holt
Hill

Hamperley

Plowden

A 49

River Onny

A 489

Wistanstow

The Long Mynd
Walk B

Miles

0   ½   1   2

Craven Arms

OS 137

a prehistoric trade route to a twentieth-century playground. If Baldwin and Gerald rode here along the old Portway, they would have found that much of the hill was given over to sheep, and a few small flocks still graze the sparse grass.

At its southern end, the Long Mynd descends steeply to the River Onny and the A 489 and A 49 to Craven Arms. An alternative route is to head east from the end of the ridge and to make the descent through Forestry land to Priors Holt Hill, and then to follow the lanes to Wistanstow and the start of the long walk round the slopes of Wenlock Edge to the elaborate and elegant stones that mark the remains of the Cluniac Priory of Much Wenlock, whence Gerald's rival, Peter de Leia came to St David's.

Walk C: Wenlock Edge to Much Wenlock (OS sheets 137 and 127)

Across the A 49 from Wistanstow, a footbridge goes across the conjoined waters of Quinny Brook and Byne Brook to the path that runs the length of Wenlock Edge through broadleaf wood-lands below the steep slopes and enclosed farmlands of the hill. This path widens out as it passes Wilderhope Manor, a house managed by the National Trust which preserves many acres of Wenlock woods. There are only a few footpaths across the hill, and to reach the priory at Much Wenlock it is best to carry on through Easthope Wood and Blakeway Coppice, go across the A 48 to Homer and then turn south-east through fields to a hill-top windmill, making the gradual descent to cross an old railway line and so enter the open parkland around the priory ruins.

Wenlock Priory

The fine Prior's Lodge, built four hundred years after Peter de Leia was here, is a private residence but anyone can walk through the carefully tended grounds surrounding the ruins of the chapter house, and the extraordinarily well-preserved and elaborately lavish octagonal washing-place in the cloister, which were both in use when Baldwin and Gerald passed by on their circuitous route to Ludlow.

Wenlock was always a wealthy foundation, as the intricate arches of the stone-work testify. It was founded after the Conquest on the site of a seventh-century monastery, by Earl

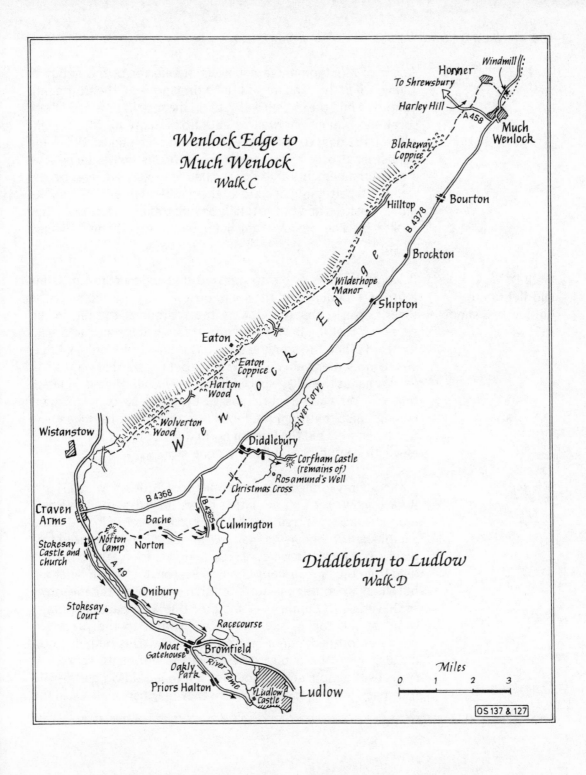

Windmill

Homer

To Shrewsbury

Harley Hill

A 458

Much Wenlock

Blakeway Coppice

**Wenlock Edge to
Much Wenlock**
Walk C

Hilltop

Bourton

B 4378

Brockton

Wilderhope Manor

Shipton

Eaton

Eaton Coppice

River Corve

Harton Wood

Wolverton Wood

W e n l o c k   E d g e

Wistanstow

Diddlebury

Corfham Castle (remains of)

Rosamund's Well

Christmas Cross

B 4368

B 4365

Craven Arms

Bache

Culmington

Stokesay Castle and church

Norton Camp

Norton

A 49

Diddlebury to Ludlow
Walk D

Onibury

Stokesay Court

Racecourse

River Teme

Moat Gatehouse

Bromfield

Oakly Park

Priors Halton

Ludlow Castle

Ludlow

Miles

0   1   2   3

OS 137 & 127

Roger of Montgomery, a generous benefactor of the abbey of Cluny when he was regent in Normandy. In the thirteenth century, when the church was rebuilt, the monks received liberal local endowments as well as gifts from Henry III, who bought himself the right to stay at the priory and even had casks of wine sent from Bristol to be stored there for his convenience. The king's arrangements strike a secular note echoed now by the delightful patterning of some of the medieval floor tiles that are still in position and by the totally absurd topiary creatures – they look a bit like bears – which fill the space of the vanished cloisters.

Walk D: Diddlebury to Ludlow (OS sheet 137)

It would be reasonable to imagine that Baldwin resumed his journey to Ludlow and the south by following the course of the River Corve, probably following the contour of the hill in the same way that the B 4378 now runs through Shipton. There is no footpath along the south eastern escarpment of Wenlock Edge, so the modern traveller has no choice but to take that way too, at least as far as the village of Diddlebury (508854). Here is a church that was old when Baldwin passed by, although only an expert could realise that from the look of its exterior. It has been very much restored, but the interior north wall of the nave still retains eleventh-century Saxon herring-bone stonework.

Stokesay

Diddlebury formed part of the manor of Corfham, which Henry II gave to Walter Clifford, father of his mistress, the fair Rosamund. A well by the site of the fine border castle which Clifford established still bears her name. The castle is now reduced to a grassy, primrose-strewn bank, reached by a footpath across the field from the lane running down to Peaton. It is worth a detour, but the main route runs north to the river through the meadows of Corvedale to Culmington and then due west past the Roman camp at the top of the hill above Norton to the preserved medieval fortified manor house of Stokesay. This building, now on display to the public, dates from the thirteenth century. It replaces the more serious fortification that Baldwin and Gerald rode past, but the church in which they may have paused in the course of their journey was built around 1150, and the tower and chancel have survived the destruction of the Civil War and the subsequent seventeenth-century rebuilding.

The country round these parts is heavily farmed and enclosed, *Bromfield* but there is a footpath to Stokesay Court, where the main road crosses the river and goes under the railway line by Onibury. From that village the lane runs south-east to Ludlow racecourse. Here it is possible to cross the track again, rejoin the A 49 and come to the remains of 'the little cell of Bromfield'. Indeed the most startling sight in this tiny village is the magnificent half-timbered gatehouse, sadly in need of urgent restoration, which once spanned the entrance to the Benedictine priory, to which Gerald was referring. It had been founded some thirty years before Baldwin's visit.

The chancel arch of the present parish church, and some ruins in the churchyard are all that remain of that small monastic settlement, affiliated to Gerald's *Alma Mater* of St Peter's at Gloucester. At the Dissolution the priory church became a private dwelling, and it was not re-consecrated until 1658. A few years later the ceiling was adorned with a gaudily vulgar painting of nubile angels tossing texts around like streamers – a fair-ground touch that has happily been preserved.

From Bromfield, the way to Ludlow goes across a tributary of *Ludlow* the Teme, past a derelict watermill to the grounds of Oakly Park. Just north of Priors Halton a footpath goes to the woods above the Teme, and skirts them to join the lane leading to the bridge beneath Gerald's 'noble castle of Ludlow', flanked by the twelfth-century market place of this much-visited medieval town.

Ludlow Castle dominating the cliffs above the river was added to until the end of the sixteenth century, so the imposing ruins which await today's tourists relate to a building even more magnificent than the fortification that Gerald saw and praised, which had been built some twenty years after the Conquest. Sated as he must have been with the proliferation of border castles, only Ludlow is given any special mention in Gerald's

Itinerary. It was the last place that he mentioned in any detail at all, for he concluded the account of his long journey most abruptly. After leaving Ludlow they went 'through Leominster to Hereford, leaving on our right hand the districts of Melenyth and Elvel: thus (describing as it were a circle) we came to the same point from which we had commenced this laborious journey through Wales'.

Hereford

So they must have ridden due south into Hereford, crossing the Roman road that runs from the River Lugg to the Roman town by Kenchester to the north-west of the city. Perhaps Bishop William de Vere rode out to welcome and congratulate the Archbishop in the open country now taken up by Hereford's racecourse, and conduct him back to the palace by the red sandstone cathedral. His effigy in the Lady chapel there shows a gentle, bearded man who would have had sympathy for the hardships that his fellow prelates must have suffered on their laborious journey.

CHAPTER NINE

Afterwards

At the end of his *Itinerary*, written some two or three years after the Archbishop's tour of Wales, Gerald summed up the results of that enterprise:

> During this long and laudable legation, about three thousand men were signed with the cross; well skilled in the use of arrows and lances, and versed in military matters; impatient to attack the enemies of the faith; profitably and happily engaged for the service of Christ, if the expedition of the Holy Cross had been forwarded with an alacrity equal to the diligence and devotion with which the forces were collected.

The Third Crusade was to end in disaster, but in the spring of 1189, hopes were still high as Baldwin, Gerald and Rannullf de Glanville, the three men who had set out from Hereford together at the beginning of the previous Lent, crossed to France on their way to the Holy Land. The Archbishop had every reason to expect that his compulsively scribbling companion would chronicle the history of Saladin's defeat and the Christian triumph in Jerusalem. It was a book never to be written, for after only a few weeks of setting out, Gerald found himself back in Britain.

He never got further than France, for the whole expedition soon started to collapse. Both Baldwin and Gerald had visions of some awful portent and, early in June, Henry II died in Chinon. The direction of the Crusade passed to the king's rebellious son Richard, a man of thirty-seven, so devoted to deeds of chivalry in the Holy Land, that he was reluctant to be distracted in any way by the affairs of his kingdom at home. So he was all too willing to listen to Baldwin's advice that Gerald and Peter de Leia should be sent back to attend to the constant troubles in Wales during the English king's absence.

Although Gerald agreed to that decision, he does not seem to have been entirely happy about it. He departed for Dieppe in an anxious state, fearful that he would lose his money, the letters that Richard had given him, and above all his own notebooks, for, as he wrote later, 'The loss of a book still to be published which those note-books contained, was not to be repaired, since (and it was that which grieved him most) the toil he had spent on them could not be repeated either by himself or any other.'

His fears were not to be realised. Both he and de Leia arrived safely in Dover, and were immediately absolved from their vows to join the Crusade. The grounds for Gerald's release were extremely dubious, for he was excused from going to the Holy Land on account of poverty, age and physical weakness, all factors which applied far more to the gentle Archbishop than to the tough archdeacon, still in his prime and due to live into his late seventies.

Baldwin sailed from Marseilles, and reached the coast of the Holy Land at Acre, where the Crusaders planned to set up the base for their attack on Jerusalem. In 1190, he died during the Saracen siege of the strange complex of underground fortifications that the Knights of St John had built there.

Back in Britain, Gerald was renewing his life's ambition to become Bishop of St David's. He was offered the bishoprics of Bangor and Llandaff as those sees became vacant, but he firmly refused to be side-tracked from his main objective. To further that, he kept himself as much as possible in the public eye, and his self-promotion led him into strange avenues. In 1191, the monks of Glastonbury claimed that they had found the tomb of Arthur and Guinevere in the cemetery by the south wall of their abbey. Two years later, the Abbot, Henry de Sully, asked Gerald to look at the skeletons and give his opinion about the authenticity of the monks' discovery. Gerald, fascinated by Merlin and the whole matter of Arthurian romance, was only too happy to agree that the once-and-future king was indeed laid in Somerset soil, and to equate the rich monastic settlement of Glastonbury, surrounded by the swamps of an inland sea, with the legendary Avalon.

Gerald had another connection with Somerset. One of his greatest friends and spiritual advisers was the gentle and saintly Hugh, prior of the Charterhouse of Witham near Frome, a monastery to which he returned annually after his appointment as Bishop of Lincoln in 1186. Six years later, it seems probable that Gerald was in Lincoln, and that it was from the college attached to that cathedral that he wrote his report on the Glastonbury tomb. By then, possibly because of his intense and scornful dislike of Richard I's Archbishop and Justicar, Hubert Walter, he had left public affairs, and was spending his time studying and lecturing in Lincoln's School of Theology. It was certainly from there in 1197 that he wrote his treatise on church reform for the clergy of his archdeaconry of Brecon.

The following year everything changed. On July 16th, Peter de Leia died, and immediately the canons of St David's approached Archbishop Hubert with the names of four candidates for the vacant bishopric. Three came from Wales. They were Gerald; Walter, Abbot of St Dogmaels; and Peter, Abbot of Whitland. The fourth was an Englishman, quickly discounted, de Leia's nephew, Reginald Foliot, an effeminate, fawning creature not above trying to win the bishopric by bribing the king. At first Gerald made out that he was disinclined to accept the nomination. He wrote to Archbishop Hubert explaining that he wished to spend the rest of his days in studious retirement. It was a face-saving move for he was rightly certain that if the matter was left to Hubert Walter, his appointment would never be ratified, and nor would that of any man so closely connected with the princes of Wales, for that country was again in a state of turmoil and revolt following the death of the Lord Rhys in the previous year. The Archbishop made his position clear when he responded to the Welsh attack on the Norman stronghold of Painscastle by ordering a mass excommunication of the survivors of the uprising. His own choice for the see of St David's was Geoffrey de Henlawe, prior of

Llanthony, a man scorned by Gerald for being more learned in medicine than theology.

In 1199, the chapter of St David's was summoned to attend the king in Normandy. Two representatives went to France only to find that Richard had been killed in the fighting at Limoges. The new king, John, was then at Chinon. He agreed to accept Gerald's appointment; he had after all known the man since the expedition to Ireland which they had undertaken together in 1185, when Henry II had chosen the archdeacon to be his son's companion 'because he was an honest and prudent man'. However nothing was to be ratified until after the coronation. That took place in Westminster Abbey on Ascension Day, and immediately afterwards Gerald, sure of his new position, was urged to start procedures which would liberate the church in Wales from the authority of Canterbury. He set out first to Ireland to seek advice on the action he should take. It was a foolish move. While he was away, John, at the mercy of his anti-Welsh advisers had serious second thoughts about Gerald's appointment. He ordered the chapter of St David's to annul his nomination and appoint his Justicar's protégé, Geoffrey de Henlawe.

Angered at this move, the chapter wrote directly to Rome demanding that Gerald's election be ratified by the Pope. This was not enough for the furious Gerald, who determined to plead his cause personally with Innocent III. Before crossing the water he rode to Manorbier to see his favourite brother, Philip. It was to be their last meeting. By August he was retracing some of the journey he had taken in 1188, riding back to Strata Florida, hoping to leave his books in safe keeping with the Cistercians. From there he rode east through the desert of rolling hills to Abbey Cwmhir, and so entered England from Kerry, where years before, when he had hoped to be elected to St David's in his uncle's place, he had rigorously held out against the claim of Bishop Adam of St Asaph. For Adam had wanted the newly re-dedicated church of Kerry to be assigned to his diocese.

The memory of the events of Michaelmas 1176 must have been in Gerald's mind as he rode past that church on his mission to Rome. Twenty-three years ago he had ordered all the bells there to be tolled in token that Kerry belonged to St David's and as a warning to Bishop Adam not to enter his territory. Ignoring the protests of a mere archdeacon, who awaited him in the church flanked by candle-holding clergy, the mitred Bishop advanced to the church door. There the two prelates solemnly pronounced edicts of excommunication upon each other.

On that occasion Gerald was the winner. All the people of Kerry were on his side and Bishop Adam was forced into an ignominious retreat. The memory of that victory must surely have warmed Gerald's heart as he made his way diagonally across England to Sandwich and the crossing to Flanders, for the wars in Normandy prevented him from taking the more direct way through France.

In Burgundy, he joined the main trade route and travelled to Rome in the company of merchants and pilgrims. He arrived at the end of November and immediately sought audience with Innocent III, then in the second year of his papacy. All over Christmas and New Year he pleaded his cause, refuting the letters sent to the Pope by Archbishop Hubert Walter. And he made time for wider issues, defending the rights of the Church of Wales and putting forward his case for the canonisation of the hermit, Caradoc. In the welter of all that business, he did not neglect to publicise his own work, presenting the Pope with copies of his books. The gift was well received, for 'the Pope, who was most learned and loved literature, kept all these books together by his bedside for about a month and used to display their elegant and pithy phrases to the Cardinals who visited him, and finally gave all save one to different Cardinals who asked for them. But the *Gemma Ecclesiastica*, which he loved beyond the rest, he would not suffer to be parted from.'

Gerald's eventual return to Britain was sad. He was greeted by the news that his beloved brother Philip had died, and he hurried to Manorbier to mourn at the grave. In the spring of 1201 he set out for Rome again. These further conversations with the Pope were inconclusive, but he had a somewhat happier homecoming. This time he learnt that both Llewellyn the Great, prince of North Wales, now a powerful young man of twenty-five, together with the prior of the holy island of Bardsey, were fully pledged to his support. He needed that encouragement, for he also discovered that on the excuse of complaints levied by Robert, Bishop of Bangor, he had been temporarily deprived of both his arch-deaconry and his home at Llanddew. Moreover he had been declared such a threat to the peace of the realm, that the Cistercian houses throughout Wales were forbidden to offer him any hospitality, or even to provide him with a guide through the wild and trackless country.

He had no alternative but to return to Rome. He crossed to Paris in November 1202 and after a hard winter journey was lodged in the Lateran by January. This time the talks lasted three months, at the end of which time, Innocent withdrew all hope of support for Gerald's claim. So, for the last time, a saddened man, he made the journey north. He was now approaching sixty and beginning to feel his age. His costly travels had left him so impoverished that he could only afford the cheapest horses, miserable, scraggy mounts; yet their rider was still recognisable by his proud bearing and the signature of his distinctive, shaggy eyebrows. At Chatillon-sur-Seine he had the indignity of being thrown into prison as a penniless subject of the English king, and was forced to spend twenty-four hours without sleep or food until he was saved from his predicament by the arrival of the Seneschal of Burgundy, who spoke out on his behalf. After that humiliating adventure he travelled slowly through France, find-ing help where he could and arriving back in England in the August.

His struggles to realise his life's ambition were at an end. When he was informed that Geoffrey de Henlawe of Llanthony had indeed been appointed to St David's, he told his arch-enemy, Hubert Walter, that he would give his consent rather than be found 'obstinate and unceasing in my opposition'. It was the end of his clerical career. The only living that he held in the last years of his life was that of rector of Chesterton, now a suburb of Bicester, but then a rich and important parish, which also supported a richly endowed resident vicar.

Gerald spent most of his time in Lincoln, writing his autobiography, and completing further books on state-craft and church reform, two of which, De *Principe Instructione* and the *Speculum Ecclesiae* contain references to the finding of Arthur's body in Glastonbury. Seventeen of the books that he wrote have survived in various forms, and there is evidence to suggest that this was by no means the whole of his literary output.

Had he achieved his ambition and become Bishop of St David's his last years would have been well chronicled and everybody would know the site of his tomb. As it is, no one even knows the exact date of his death and his burial place is a mystery. The living at Chesterton became vacant in 1223, so it is reasonable to assume that he was no longer alive in that year. There is an almost legendary tradition that he came back to Manorbier to die, and Richard Fenton, the nineteenth-century historian of Pembrokeshire, believed that he was indeed buried at St David's. Yet it seems more likely that his bones lie in Lincoln, where he spent his last days. As an old man, he must have taken pleasure in the north rose window which still graces that cathedral, and rejoiced at the canonisation, in 1220, of Bishop Hugh, his old friend and mentor. Perhaps he even took a part in planning the major rebuilding of the eastern part of the cathedral, where the saint's shrine was to be housed, although that work was not to be completed until 1280.

It is impossible to believe that he died entirely forgotten. In any case, posterity has reason to be grateful that his ambition was not realised. As Bishop of St David's he could never have penned the books that have given readers through the centuries such a lively understanding of the troubled times he lived in and the enduring nature of his grandmother's country. And if Sir Richard Colt Hoare of Stourhead in the county of Wiltshire had not lost his wife at an early age, he might never have gone on his extensive travels and developed that abiding love of Wales which led him to translate Gerald's *Itinerarium Kambriae* into English, thereby taking it out of the realm of esoteric scholarship and giving it to the general reader.

The tragedy at the core of the lives of Gerald and Sir Richard can be likened to the despair that many people must have felt at the failure of the Third Crusade. When Gerald came to contemplate that disaster, he was led to consider how often good may come out of affliction, and to quote the sixth-century Pope Gregory, who wrote an epistle on the matter, concluding 'For who does not know how fortunate a circumstance it was that Paul went to Italy, and suffered so dreadful a ship-wreck? But the ship of his heart remained unbroken amidst the waves of the sea.'

Index

Page numbers in *italic* refer to the maps